THE CUSTOMER-CENTRIC YOU

For a complete list of Management Books 2000 titles
visit our web-site on http://www.mb2000.com

THE CUSTOMER-CENTRIC YOU

*Making customers the focus of
everything you do*

Stephen Hewett

(Illustrations by Ed Young)

2000

First published in 2011 by Management Books 2000 Ltd
Forge House, Limes Road
Kemble, Cirencester
Gloucestershire, GL7 6AD, UK
Tel: 0044 (0) 1285 771441
Fax: 0044 (0) 1285 771055
Email: info@mb2000.com
Web: www.mb2000.com

British Library Cataloguing in Publication Data is available

ISBN 9781852526726

CONTENTS

Too often, as customers, we are put through processes that are not focused on us as individuals. This leaves us feeling frustrated and complaining loudly to whoever will listen. But the good news is that it works the other way too. The more that organisations respect us as customers and the more that organisations organise themselves around us and our agenda, the better our customer experience will be and the more we will feel appreciated.

As for organisations, if they make us feel like this they will have a much better chance of sustained success.

Luke Mayhew,
Chairman, British Retail Consortium.

ACKNOWLEDGEMENTS

My sincere thanks to all the people in my life who help me enjoy being customer-centric. These people include my wife Carolyn, my daughter Dee, my son Alex, my son-in-law James and, youngest but certainly not least, my grandson Aaron. I also draw much inspiration from my colleagues at Charteris, especially David Pickering, Martin Chitty, Kevin Waters, Jeremy Labram, Graham Simmons and Alan Miles; and from my Charteris clients, particularly Sue Redmond, corporate director of community services at Wiltshire Council. Sue has greatly contributed to my thinking on customer-centricity.

From my days at the John Lewis Partnership, I would like to extend my thanks to Luke Mayhew and to Andrew McMillan, a Charteris colleague. From my aviation days, my gratitude to David Fairclough and to George Ward, whose business interests include being chairman of Bonusprint.

In the UK, my sincere gratitude to Mark Price, managing director of Waitrose; Steve Lewis, chief executive of Majestic Wine; Christina Patterson; the financial services industry entrepreneur Rob Farbrother; the writer and historian Paul Crampton; Professor David Thomson and David Howlett of MMR Research; and Donna Morrison, public relations manager of Majestic Wine. In New York, my thanks to Maggie Porges of Laforce + Stevens, the public relations consultancy of Dale Carnegie Training, and to Dale Carnegie Training itself and especially to Muriel Goldstein.

My thanks also at Charteris to Catherine Edmondson and Georgina Stamp.

My thanks to Paul Crampton for kindly allowing me to quote from his novel *Ronnie Darwin was my uncle*, published by Pen Press Publishers Limited in 2006.

I would in addition like to thank James Essinger for his comprehensive assistance and talents, Margaret Dowley MBE for her insight and for her help with text production, Ed Young for the illustrations and Jane Young for all her help. I hope you like Ed's illustrations as much as I do.

My special thanks to Imogen Chitty, our youngest contributor. May the world you inherit, Imogen, be ever more customer-centric.

Finally, my sincere gratitude to my publisher, Nick Dale-Harris, for his enthusiastic response to our initial approaches and for all his help and guidance since then, and for thinking of the highly appropriate sub-title.

Stephen Hewett

FOREWORD

by Mark Price, Managing Director, Waitrose

I was delighted when Stephen Hewett asked me to write a Foreword for this book.

At one level, I've great pleasure in contributing to a friend's creative project. I've known Stephen for twenty years; we were colleagues at John Lewis and worked together there on many exciting and deeply engaging assignments.

At another level, Stephen's philosophy of customer-centricity – that it is a vitally important attitude to build into your personal take on the world as much as in your professional life – is in harmony with my own philosophy.

Customer-centricity really *is* the core of business. Indeed, it could be seen as the essence of life itself. None of us could survive as babies if others didn't care about our agenda and put our needs before their own. Parents realise that this selflessness is a fundamental part of bringing up children, but it's too easy to forget that – as Stephen explains – we have customers in *all* aspects of our lives and they all need our attention.

In our professional lives, of course, we need to keep our customers happy, by offering them what they want, if we are to make a living. But – as *The Customer-Centric You* makes profoundly clear – it's not enough just to have a grudging desire to think about customers because you worry that if you don't you won't make a living.

Customers deserve better than that from you, just as the people you love deserve more than a grudging kind of love.

One reason customers deserve better from you is because they are entitled to the very best attention from the organisations that compete to win their loyalty. Another reason is – as Stephen argues so forcefully in this book – that you will be infinitely more fulfilled, satisfied and happy in your life when you are genuinely switched on to the agenda of others, and have learned to care about that agenda because you want to care about it.

Stephen is a customer guru for our times. His articulate meshing of strategic organisational demands with inspiring thinking on personal development, blended with exciting and thought-provoking philosophy, makes *The Customer-Centric You* a tremendous read.

Stephen readily acknowledges that his fifteen years at the John Lewis Partnership (JLP) have played a vital role in making his thinking on customer-centricity what it is.

In the Partnership we arrive at doing the right thing for customers by thinking of our Partners (our employees) first. Our ultimate purpose, as set out by our founder, is the happiness of Partners through their worthwhile and satisfying employment in a successful business. Our Partners share the responsibilities and rewards of ownership and are dedicated to serving our customers.

So you could most certainly say that our Partners have customer-centricity running through them. Any organisation that wants to have customer-centricity in its DNA must find its own way of motivating staff to believe in customer-centricity and to be passionate about carrying it out every day.

I think it very significant, by the way, that Stephen pinpoints retail as an industry whose fundamental nature has changed little over the years and which has much the same customer-centricity imperative no matter what technology is brought to the industry.

Many of the great retail organisations of the nineteenth century are still flourishing today, and seeking to win the hearts of customers in the age of the internet and the space shuttle much as they did in the age of the telegraph and the steam locomotive.

Stepping right into the present, the importance of customer-centricity is even greater during a time of economic challenges. I'm proud that during times when the economy has presented such challenges, both divisions of JLP – Waitrose and John Lewis – have performed strongly.

That said, part of being truly devoted to customer-centricity means avoiding complacency. You can never know too much about what your customers need, and you can never stop finding the best ways to meet those needs.

As for me, I want Waitrose customers to have a great experience every time they shop with us, whether it's to buy everyday essentials, a terrific bottle of wine to go with a dinner party, the food for the dinner party, an entire weekly shop, or whatever else. I want the service we give them to be first-rate and memorable, every time.

And this is the whole point. After all the anecdotes in this entertaining and thought-provoking book, after all the clear and original thinking it contains, customer-centricity is, in the end, only real when you, yourself, put it into practice.

I know Stephen will agree with me that putting customer-centricity into practice is what this book is all about.

PREFACE

The Customer-Centric You is about how we can all become better at our relationships with customers, no matter how good we might think we are at this now.

My fundamental point is this: you can't improve your relationships with your customers in any meaningful sense by just following a set of guidelines.

After all, as a matter of pure logic, if customer-centricity *was* something you could just install by loading a program or following a set procedure, everyone would have it and there would be little or no need for me to write this book. But the very fact that many customers are frequently dissatisfied, if not extremely dissatisfied, with the level of service they receive proves that customer-centricity is very far indeed from being something that everyone has.

Ultimately, customer-centricity is delivered not by an organisation but by the people who work for it.

As Mark Price, praising the people at the John Lewis Partnership, says in his Foreword, any organisation that wants to have customer-centricity in its DNA needs to rely on its staff to believe in customer-centricity and to be passionate about carrying it out every day.

This may seem like an obvious remark, and in a sense it is, but it is also a profound one with wide-ranging implications.

The biggest implication of all is this: personal attitude of staff who interact with customers is of prime importance if customer-centricity is to be delivered.

A comment made by Steve Lewis, chief executive of Majestic Wine and quoted in the interview with him that appears later in the book, seems to me to say it all. As Steve says:

I don't think you can teach people to be charming. You can teach people to follow certain procedures, but charm is something they either have or they don't. You have to be many other things too, in this business – driven, focused and intelligent, for example – but charm is absolutely essential and without it I don't think we can make someone into an employee we'd be happy to employ or – and of course this is an extremely important point too – who'd be likely to be happy to work for us.

Yes, delivering true customer-centricity indeed requires charm... and sincerity.

Merely pursuing a set of guidelines for being customer-centric would have about the same relationship to a real, deep, organic skill at relating to customers and a desire to do your very best for them, as painting by numbers does to real art.

No... all of us, if we are really going to improve how we relate to our customers, need to be charming in how we deal with customers, and sincere, and we need to care about the agenda of customers very sincerely.

Very often, no matter how good we might think we are at dealing with customers now, we can only be all we need to be for our customers if we *rethink ourselves*.

We also need to take steps to ensure that, once we *have* re-thought ourselves, we can remain in touch with our re-thought selves through all the bad times of discouragement, exhaustion, worries, and unforeseen disasters.

But if we can do that, if we can rethink ourselves and stay in touch with our new selves throughout everything that life throws at us, we will truly be all we can be as businesspeople *and* as people in the widest sense.

And the main beneficiary of our new selves – though by no means the only beneficiary – will, in fact, be *us*.

Yes, because *you* are your most important customer of all. By tuning yourself to the agenda of the people in your life who are your other customers, you'll also become more interested in life, more engaged by it, more fascinated by our wondrous world, more successful in your career, and even happier than you've ever been before, even if (which I very much hope), you're happy already.

In fact, being customer-centric is especially important when your life is difficult: whether or not the difficulties you are going through stem completely or partly from problems at work.

Generally, and I think this is a very useful guideline to bear in mind, when our lives are difficult we tend to act in a more selfish way, but on the whole we are more likely so solve our problems if we become *less* selfish and focus more on the agenda of other people. To take just one instructive example, J.K. Rowling was an unemployed and poverty-stricken single mum, close (as she herself admits) to being clinically depressed, when she began writing the first Harry Potter story. By focusing on the agenda of other people, and giving them a great story to read, she totally transformed her life for ever... and reinvigorated the reading habits of young people worldwide into the bargain.

Ultimately, I want *The Customer-Centric You* to make you feel, every morning, utterly positive, and completely full of the maximum energy and passion to do your best for your customers.

More specifically, I want *The Customer-Centric You* to make you feel warm and refreshed and full of new plans and idea for how you can bring to the lives of all the customers in your life what they most want from you... as well as new things you can offer them that they hadn't even thought of.

As for you, you are, among many other things, my customer and I'll do my best to bring all the above benefits to you when you read my book.

What you do with my ideas and suggestions is, of course, up to you.

I'll also try to make sure we have plenty of fun along the way.

PART ONE

UNDERSTANDING
CUSTOMER-CENTRICITY

1

YOU AND YOUR CUSTOMERS

First thoughts

Dear reader, welcome to *The Customer-Centric You*.

This is a book about business, but it's more than that.

It's really a book about you.

In fact, it's a book about all of us.

It's about all of us because its subject-matter is this: *the things we need to do to make others like – and ideally love – whatever it is we're offering them.*

I really do mean 'whatever it is', whether this is some product or service we want to sell, or the *idea* of ourselves as supplying something to others – whether that something is the skills needed to carry out a particular project or assignment, or the experience and competence to make a success of a new position within an organisation, or even something personal – such as love in a romantic or family relationship.

As for who the other people to whom you're offering what you are offering, this really can be anyone. It might even be the entire population of a nation to whom you're offering your services as prime minister or president. After all, even prime ministers or presidents have customers: the electorate.

As you'll already have realised, the subject-matter of *The Customer-Centric You* doesn't stop at your professional life. Yes, this book is about that, but it's also about your relationship with your customers – customers in the widest sense of the word – meaning *everyone* who matters to you.

This, of course, is a much broader definition of 'customer' than the usual one, which focuses on the customer of an organisation that's delivering some product or service. But the broader definition is a thoroughly *logical* definition. The truth is that you have customers in *all* aspects of your life, not only in your professional life.

Admittedly, you wouldn't guess that if you looked at the dictionary definition of 'customer'. The Shorter Oxford English Dictionary, for example, defines 'customer' as:

> *a person who makes a purchase or gives business, especially to any particular seller or establishment.*

But we shouldn't blame the dictionary. Dictionaries merely record usage. The dictionary definition of 'customer' is the most usual definition: the one that everyone recognises and uses.

Yet the curious thing is that, from the late Middle Ages to the early seventeenth century, there *was* another definition of customer in popular use: it meant an associate or companion. This meaning of the word 'customer' is, however, obsolete in English today, except in the narrow sense of an opponent in some sport with whom one regularly plays: we sometimes hear the word 'customer' used to mean that. You'll doubtless also have noticed that the word is sometimes used to mean an opponent whom one regularly *beats*.

You may ask: why, here in *The Customer-Centric You*, do we need a wider definition of the notion of the customer? What's wrong with the usual definition?

Well, I think here are two things wrong with it.

Firstly, the usual definition doesn't cover public sector organisations, where the customer does not make a purchase in any traditional sense. Yes, the public sector organisation's costs will be paid for by taxes, but it is by no means necessarily the case that the person who is receiving the service from the public sector organisation will be a taxpayer. Indeed, in the case of certain social welfare services, it is in fact fairly unlikely to be the case that the recipient of the services will currently be paying taxes.

Public sector organisations are increasingly (and, in my view, quite rightly) referring to the people they serve in a particular community as 'customers', even though these people are, clearly, customers in a very different sense to, say, the customers of a bank or a butcher's shop.

Secondly, more than thirty years of earning my living from helping people forge better relationships with their customers has convinced me that in order to improve how we deal with customers in our professional lives, we need to improve how we deal with people in *all* areas of our lives. We need to rethink how we deal with people generally. The approach simply has to be holistic as well as sincere. Anything less will not work.

Indeed, the truth is that, at an overall level, if we are to make the most of ourselves in every respect, we must continually refine our skill at interacting with people, and this applies to the people in our personal lives as much as to those in our professional lives. If we don't continually refine our skill, we are likely soon to find ourselves as much without good friends and good personal relationships as we are likely to be without commercial customers.

That great eighteenth-century literary gentleman and practical philosopher, the legendary Dr Samuel Johnson, once observed:

If a man does not make new acquaintance as he advances through life, he will soon find himself left alone. A man... should keep his friendship in constant repair.

And he was, as usual, right. Equally to the point, what applies to friendship generally applies to customers generally: that is, all the customers in your life. We all need to keep our relationships with our customers, in every area of our lives, in a constant state of repair.

Because of the above reasons, we absolutely need a broader definition of 'customer' here in *The Customer-Centric You* than the usual one found in the dictionary and employed in common parlance. I hope you agree that we've already reached the point of no return to our old, limited ways of thinking about who customers are.

I propose the following as a suitable broader definition:

A customer is any person, anywhere and in any capacity, whom you want to influence to want what you are offering them.

Notice that the definition is about you wanting to influence someone to *want* what you are offering them.

Merely influencing someone to *like* what you are offering them is not enough. No-one is going to buy something from you merely because they like it; they have to feel they need it, and they are only going to part with their hard-earned cash to buy what you are offering them if they really *do* feel they need it, either because they need it at a practical level (such as a vital spare part for some domestic appliance), or because they need it in order to feel good in the way that they want to feel. This might apply, for example, to a favourite food product, drink product or some other product that they regard as bound up with the quality of their life.

This really is what this book is all about: what you need to do to make people want what you have to offer them.

Go about this the right way, and the world will beat a path to your front door.

Similarly, no-one is going to become romantically involved with you only because they like you (well, maybe not unless you are very rich and famous, anyway). They have to want you in every sense, not only in the rather narrow sexual sense the word 'want' has acquired in this context. As for members of your family such as your children, what you want them to want from you is (probably) your love.

This broader definition of the customer has the advantage of being flexible, and infinitely extensible. Use it, and suddenly our whole understanding of the customer becomes different, more alive, more exciting... and more likely to lead to specific and definite benefits for the customer.

As for 'what you are offering them' (i.e. your customers), that really can be *anything*.

In your professional lives, depending on what you do for a living, your customers might be, to take just a few of a myriad examples:

- a housewife (or home-husband) if you're a butcher selling meat
- a commercial organisation or private individual if you're a computer software designer selling software
- a school, college or university tutor if you're a student writing an essay
- a person in need of home help if you work for the social care department of a local council
- a voter if you're a politician
- a book reader if you're a novelist writing books
- a music lover if you're a musician
- a myriad other types of customers for a correspondingly myriad of other types of professional activity.

And, naturally, the role the particular customer plays in relation to you at any one time is only how they might relate to *you*: they will be other types of customers to other people during the same day, and indeed during the same hour.

It's hardly too great a stretch to imagine that one person could, even during just one day, buy meat, buy computer software, mark an essay, need home help from the local council, vote, buy a book and buy some music.

And these are only your customers in your professional lives. Of course, you have personal customers as well: by this I mean 'customers' using the broader definition I've just suggested. What you offer your personal customers might include: your friendship, your love, your support, your guidance, and your attention generally in all kinds of ways.

It's useful to note at this point that in your professional life you will mostly be wooing people who are *strangers*, at least to start with.

Even when you have a good and fairly reliable customer base, you are likely to be wooing strangers much of the time, or else there will certainly be (or at least there should be) people in your organisation whose role involves doing that. That wooing is, of course, the basis of much of the world's commercial activity, alongside the actual provision of services to customers.

In your personal life, though, you spend most of your time interacting with people who, by definition, are *not* strangers: your spouse or life partner, friends and family for example.

That said, some of them are at some point.

That particular moment when you meet a stranger whom you want to be special in your life is too major a moment for me not to hand over the stage to those wonderfully talented gentlemen Richard Rodgers (composer) and Oscar Hammerstein (lyricist) who between them wrote the enchanting song *Some Enchanted Evening*.

> *Some enchanted evening, you may see a stranger,*
> *You may see a stranger, across a crowded room.*
> *And somehow you know, you know even then*
> *That someday you'll see her again and again.*

But of course after that moment of your enchanted evening you will want the person to be anything *but* a stranger.

The same is true in your professional life: you don't want a prospective new customer to be a stranger for long. The difference is that in your professional life you are likely to be meeting 'potential-customers-who-are-strangers' very often, whereas in your personal life it will (probably) be a slightly rarer event.

I'm not, by the way, saying that you shouldn't care about strangers you meet in your non-professional life. Anyone living in any type of society is going to encounter strangers fairly regularly who want their help, whether it's someone in the street asking for loose change, an old man who seems to need your help crossing the road (though let's first make sure he actually *wants* to cross the road), or if you are, say, first on the scene at an accident.

But these interactions are not – according to my definition above – interactions with customers. For an interaction to qualify under the definition, there has to be some element of self-interest in the transaction: there has to be something you are offering the person that you want the person to want.

Giving some loose change to someone begging on the street, helping an old man across the road, assisting someone who has just suffered an accident, are all purely altruistic acts, and the people are not customers.

Why focusing on customers involves your entire personality

I began *The Customer-Centric You* by saying that while it was a book about business, it was also more than that.

I'll go further. I want to say that it is extremely difficult, if not close to impossible, for anyone to become truly customer-centric if they see themselves as having two essentially distinct personas: their business persona and their 'personal life' persona.

Most business books do indeed seem to assume that you have a 'business persona' (which the business books target in their tutoring activities), and also a more general persona, which they usually ignore.

Self-help books are directed at the reader's entire personality, but most business books are aimed only at the 'business' side of the reader's mindset.

True, there are exceptions: Mark McCormack's excellent and

deservedly successful *What They Don't Teach You at Harvard Business School* is one. McCormack, in his book — which is a handy collection of pithy nuggets of practical and tried and tested business advice — takes for granted that he is seeking to modify the reader's personality in a general sense, not only the reader's attitude to business.

Generally, though, business books do tend to be directed at the 'business' side of one's thinking and personality, as if that were something entirely distinct from who one is in a more holistic sense.

This attitude makes no sense whatsoever to me.

The demonstrable fact of the matter is that in these times of ours, more than any other time in history, the rigid demarcation between one's professional or business persona and one's personal persona is blurring. Assuming, of course, that the polarisation was ever a valid one in the first place, which actually I doubt.

There are many reasons for this blurring. These reasons include:

The changing nature of work

Ultimately, the most important reason for the blurring of professional and personal roles arises from the changing nature of work itself.

The time was that after leaving school or further or higher education, people 'got a job' with a particular organisation in a particular sector, and tended to stay with that organisation, or at least in that sector, for most or all of their lives.

True, the idea of the 'job for life' was always a bit of a fantasy; jobs have always been to some extent precarious; but there's no doubt that, in the past, individuals' careers tended to be substantially focused mostly around specific organisations or sectors.

Of course, this remains to some extent true today, but for more and more people, jobs tend to be increasingly *project-based*.

Typically, you're hired to undertake a specific project or sets of projects, and your performance in that respect is going to determined whether you keep on being employed, or whether you are given other projects to do.

This trend has gone hand-in-hand with – and has doubtless partly been furthered by – burgeoning competition in most sectors, including cross-border *and* cross-sector competition. Much less is sacred in professional life today than was ever the case in the past. This greatly reduced sacredness has gone hand-in-hand with a much greater informality of manner and dress style in the world of business and other areas of professional life.

Today, in the business world, everything is up for grabs. Foreign ownership of renowned domestic brands whose origins are part of business folklore? It's as commonplace as foreign ownership of major domestic utilities suppliers. Wars have in the past been fought to stop such major commercial national assets from passing into foreign ownership, but the chequebook has in recent years often won what tanks, airplanes and infantry regiments could not.

Competition and the hunger for success means that, today, there are few crevices indeed within the private, for-profit, sector where employees can languish comfortably by keeping out of controversy, by not causing trouble, and by doing the very least they need to do to keep their jobs.

Instead, *everyone* has to be on their toes and to do their very best to get top-level results: that is, if they want to keep on paying their mortgage.

What's true of the private sector is, more and more true of the public sector. The days when a job in the public sector really could be a job for life are already almost gone, and soon they'll have vanished completely.

The reason for the increasing lack of indolent bolt-holes in the public sector is that governments nowadays, not unreasonably, feel that tax-payers' hard-won money needs to be spent just as efficiently as private capital. Indeed, shouldn't it be spent even more so, for doesn't every government have an elected, and moral, responsibility, to give tax-payers the very best value for money?

Indeed, I'm personally glad this is the case, because over the past few years my main professional activity has been working with a number of local councils in Britain to effect a transformation in how they look after the very people they were created to serve.

Yes, professional life is for more and more people a matter of successfully carrying out specific projects, which by extension means that your own career is more and more likely to consist of successfully carrying out a succession of projects, just as an actor or writer (say) will see their own career as a succession of hard-won acting or writing credits.

You see more and more evidence of the project-based approach to careers even at very large organisations. People's careers at such large organisations tend increasingly to be based not on working for the organisation as such, but on performing specific projects at the organisation. And, as in so many areas of professional life, you're only regarded as being as good as what you achieved in your last project.

There's a flipside to this, of course. Few people have much job security nowadays, and this is as much to do with the changing nature of work as with any economic factors.

Employees – and employers too – today need to be on their toes all the time.

Of course, the phenomenon of the increasingly project-based nature of business life today can seem unfair. Seniority counts for less than it once did, and winning a senior position at any organisation is no longer a gravy train to a comfortable and prosperous life and, in due course, a fat pension. Indeed senior people themselves are always under even more exacting pressures to perform than middle-ranking and junior employees.

As for chief executives, the general public, marvelling at chief executives' salaries, tends not to realise just how short-term many chief executives positions actually are. Three years is, in most sectors, a pretty good innings for a chief executive: mergers, acquisitions, changes in corporate strategy, private indiscretions, physical health problems or sheer burn-out conspire against chief executive professional longevity.

What does all this mean for you?

It means, by and large, is that it no longer makes sense for you to hand the responsibility for your career success to the organisation you work for.

Instead, your career is increasingly likely to consist of a 'portfolio' of professional positions and activities, very possibly including one or more spells of self-employment. It's difficult to know, in advance, just what the nature of that portfolio will be. What *is*, at least, certain is that the one central factor common to all the career positions on your portfolio will be *you*.

You, and your developing and broadening professional and personal skills.

And because it's nowadays going to be *you* who is at the heart of your own career management rather than any of the organisations you work for or work with, it makes abundant sense that you should aim to develop yourself *holistically* career-wise. This means ensuring that your entire personality, mindset, and range of skills are all involved in that development.

The practical fact of how people think

There's another key factor in the blurring between one's professional or business persona and one's personal persona. It's this: even if it were psychologically possible to present two completely different personas to the world, your 'professional life' persona and your 'personal life' persona, it would be singularly stressful to proceed in that way and no way to live.

You are one person, not two. Yes, you are who you are, and you can't escape that.

I admit: it *is* possible, when you go to work, to hang your 'leisure life personality' up in the company cloakroom and pick up a new 'work-life personality' module from your locker. But people who do this – or, which may be more to the point – people whose jobs require them to do this – are unlikely to achieve very much, at least not in that particular job. How can we ever possibly perform to our highest potential if we are not being true to ourselves? How can we possibly be all we can be if we are only giving half of ourselves? No: ideally you need a job or occupation where you can be true to yourself, and if you don't have such a job or occupation *now*, it's a fair bet that you will be restless until you find one.

The reality of how you are assessed to work on a particular project or interviewed for a particular new job

Who would ever doubt that at any interview for any job worth having, your entire personality, as much as your professional skills, is what is being scrutinised?

This is even truer if you are competing for a project as a self-employed person, or as a consultant.

Every aspiring consultant needs to be able to show evidence of possessing the right technical skills for the potential assignment in question, along with testimonials that demonstrate expertise. Yet overall, it's abundantly true that what wins new clients and projects for any self-employed person is the self-employed person's personality.

The higher you progress in your career, the more important your personality becomes compared with your technical skills

This is another reason for the increasing blurring between worklife and leisure life personas. The higher up you go in a corporate hierarchy, or the higher you ascend in any self-employed, advisory or consultancy role, the more your entire personality is what matters.

One sees this in all commercial and industrial sectors. Career progression means an emphasis on management, and management skills are always predominantly *interpersonal*.

Indeed, in almost all career paths a point will come where, if your personality does *not* win you promotion to management level and lets you succeed when you get to that level, you are likely to encounter setbacks in your career.

A successful dealer in a financial institution, for example, will sooner or later probably be invited to lead a *team* of dealers. This is by no means always an easy transition for dealers, who are likely to find that managing a team of dealers demands substantially different skills from those required to be a dealer. Similarly, technical specialists in any discipline often find the transition to management difficult.

Interestingly, chief executives of large organisations like to keep their desks clear and uncluttered. Surely this shows very explicitly that what they see themselves as really offering in their professional life is their *entire personality*, rather than their skill at dealing with bits of 'business' contained in documentation?

The very fact that the higher up an executive goes at an organisation the less cluttered their desks tend to be, confirms, I think, that the higher up one goes in business, the more one's sheer personality matters.

Increasing technological progress throughout society tends to create more jobs requiring 'personality'

If we could catapult ourselves back in time to the business world of the nineteenth century or the first thirty years or so of the twentieth, we would be amazed at the high proportion of jobs that require physical skill and sheer physical effort compared with those requiring brain-power and 'personality'.

Today, with sophisticated machines and high-tech tools performing tasks previously carried out by people, a greater and greater proportion of jobs require, above all, cerebral skills and 'personality.' This trend is continuing, which is one of many reasons why all young people should strive to get the very best education they can.

Curiously, one profession that it is hard to automate to any great degree is the operation of the physical branch of a shop. I was a retailer before I became a management consultant, and as someone who worked at the John Lewis Partnership for much of my career, I'm glad that there are limits to the extent to which the retail business can be automated. As this places more of an onus on retailers to be absolutely sincere in their approach to customers. I return to this theme in this book, as the retail business has many insights to offer regarding winning and wooing customers.

Increasing use of personal electronic tools tends to blur differences between one's business time and one's personal time

More and more people use the same personal electronic communications tools both for personal and business applications, whether for sending or receiving phone calls, text messages or emails. Similarly, they use the same personal electronic communications tools to surf the web both for personal and business uses.

Naturally, this development tends to lead to a blurring of work and leisure time.

The increase in the nature of project-based jobs that make use of the skills you most enjoy deploying tend to blur the distinction between business and personal life anyway

With more and more jobs being project-based, your career success will tend to depend more and more on how adept you become at implementing your most precious core professional skills to some practical purpose.

Other things being equal, you are unlikely to be really good at some particular skill unless you really like exercising that skill, and if you really like exercising a skill, doesn't this tend to raise the question of whether exercising it is work or pleasure?

Especially, one might add, if you like it so much that you are continually tempted to exercise the skill in the evenings or at weekend.

The best-known businesspeople exult in being the same creative and dynamic individuals at work and at play

In a business world where the cult of the business celebrity is more pronounced than it has ever been, it's significant that the business celebs we see on TV, hear on the radio, read about in the newspapers and whose blogs we might surf on the internet, not only obviously *don't* regard themselves as having a business persona as well as a more general persona, but actually positively exult in being the same business-minded, insightful, customer-sensitive person whenever they are exposed to the media.

I'm not suggesting that the personality they project to the media necessarily represents the sum total of what they're like as people. To take just one example, the world-famous businessman Richard Branson is known within the Virgin Group for his meticulous attention to the facts and figures of his various businesses. This seems a little contradictory compared with his public image as an affable, smiling, cheerfully competitive and customer-friendly chap.

The point here is that that business celebrities clearly don't regard themselves as having a business persona and a personal life persona. And if they don't, I can't see any particular reason why anyone should.

These reasons for the increased blurring of professional life with personal life all suggest that in today's business world, the idea of you having some 'business persona' that is distinct, from who you are as a person, makes no sense at all.

The very idea that such a polarisation could exist at all seems to be a hangover from the nineteenth century, when worklife and personal life *were* much more polarised, and when it was often assumed that the head of a family needed to be tough (for 'tough', read 'frequently obnoxious') at work, and could only really 'be himself' at home.

Ah... the Victorians. We'll be meeting them before long.

As we shall see, the Victorians may have something to teach us about customer focus, but not so much to teach us as they would have liked to think.

By the way, the pleasure of meeting Tobias Hardcastle, master of Hardcastle Knitwear Limited, still awaits you...

'Yes, well, hurry up, lad!' thunders Tobias.

In any event, the point, surely, is this – you, the entirety of who you are, is the person who is going to be successful, or otherwise. You really are the same person at work as you are at home or busy with your leisure life; you're just doing different things. The need to get a good handle on what the customers in your life want involves your entire personality, and your personal life as much as your professional life.

Who *are* your customers?

Now that we have the right kind of broader, working definition of the 'customer' for the purposes of this book, let's look at the question of who your customers actually *are*.

The point is, the question of who your customers are is, in fact, probably not as obvious as it may at first seem.

Of course, in some cases the identity of your customer *will* be obvious.

Looking again at the list above that gives some examples of customer relationships in the professional capacity, it's clear that if you're a butcher running a butcher's shop your customers will be the people who come into the shop to buy from you.

But if you are indeed, for example, a butcher, there'll be other kinds of people whom you will want to influence to like what you are offering them. Indeed, whatever your occupation, there will be a range of different people whom it is likely you will need to influence positively. All these people all count as customers, even though they may not seem to be 'obvious' customers.

To continue the example of the butcher, one person who is not an obvious customer of a butcher but who would nonetheless be an important person for the butcher to influence positively would be the local public health inspector, whose periodic approval of the butcher's working conditions and general hygiene in the shop would be essential if the butcher wanted to go on trading.

This is just one example of a less obvious kind of customer a butcher would have, but there are others. If you have any employees, even *they* are a kind of customer, if you think about it. After all, without them you couldn't trade, especially on days when you are ill, or on holiday, or visiting a nearby farm that supplies you with pigs. Your window-cleaner is a kind of customer, too; butchers' shops with dirty windows aren't going to do much business. Of course, your window-cleaner will, quite rightly, see *you* as a customer, in a more obvious kind of way.

Going down the list, we encounter the example of the novelist. This is an interesting example of a profession where the true nature of the customer is far from obvious. Yes, it is true at one level that a novelist's customers are his or her readers, but the clarity of the customer relationship between a novelist and the novelist's readers only becomes obvious once the novelist has won a place as an established player.

J.K. Rowling, for example, the world-famous author of the prodigiously successful Harry Potter series of books, did not sell her first book by going directly to customers. (Some authors, including first-timers, sometimes try to do this, with varying levels of success, by setting up a website.) J.K. Rowling went for the more mainstream approach. After completing her first Harry Potter book, she sent a sample of the material to a number of literary agents in the UK, including the agent Christopher Little, whom she later said she chose because she liked the sound of his name.

He, for his part, liked what she sent him, and asked to read the rest of the book on an exclusive basis. He liked that, too, and then spent a year trying to sell the book and a proposal for a series of other books.

Finally, after a frustrating year of rejections from about half a dozen publishers, the book was purchased by the UK publisher Bloomsbury, who loved it (a far-sighted editor there said it had the potential to be a classic). Bloomsbury brought the first book out, though only in an edition of 500 books designed for sale to a library. J.K. Rowling's first advance (that is, a non-returnable advance payment on royalties) for that library edition, was just £2,000, of which Christopher Little remarked to her, 'this is all very well, but it isn't going to make your fortune.' But of course she *did* end up making her fortune, and Christopher Little's too, because more and more readers loved the books and cried (literally, in many cases) for more. As for the books in that first library edition, surviving copies now change hands for more than £20,000.

Here, we see a complex three-stage customer process. J.K. Rowling's first customer was the community of literary agents, then Christopher Little became her most important customer, then Bloomsbury became a customer both of J.K. Rowling and her agent. Finally, the readers of the books became customers of J.K. Rowling, her agent and Bloomsbury, with the movie company Warner Brothers also getting involved as a customer when the films began to be made.

There are also other customers involved: book reviewers, newspaper writers (indeed the surge of the entire Harry Potter series to great success derives substantially from some very positive coverage, over a period of days, in the UK newspaper *The Daily Telegraph*), film critics and so on.

The truth of the matter is that most business situations, if you analyse them, reveal a variety of complex customer relationships that may not at first sight be at all obvious.

Another example occurs when a chain of retail shops wants to open a new store somewhere. Of course, the people who come through the doors of the completed store, to buy things, are customers, but a major retailer has many other kinds of customers to think about.

A supermarket chain, for example, will — before it can build a new store in a particular locality — need to convince many different types of customers who will very possibly never actually walk into the store if it *is* built. Examples of people it will need to convince would include local authority planning officers and local community groups. These people are customers in a very real sense; indeed, without them the chain will never get to open its store and win more conventional and obvious types of customers.

So, yes, we need to think hard about who our real customers are before we do much else of anything in relation to making the most of ourselves in our professional and personal spheres.

Generally, my aim here is to emphasise that the only really useful way to regard customers is indeed to see them as those *people, anywhere and in any capacity, whom you do indeed want to influence to want what you are offering them, whatever it may be.* And no matter how good or bad your professional day has been, you will indeed also have your customers in your personal life, when you come home or when you take part in any social activity.

Internal and external customers

It is useful to mention at this point the difference between *internal* and *external* customers in organisational life. However, the real point is that a particular person is a customer at all: any attempt precisely to categorise the type of customer they are may not be excessively helpful.

But it is worth bearing in mind that, if you work within an organisation, some of your customers will also work inside the organisation (internal customers) while others will be outside the organisation (external customers). They are also often called end-customers or end-users. I don't think it an especially good idea to regard external customers as more important than internal customers: I think the principles of customer-centricity should apply equally to all your customers. But recognising the difference between the two types of customers is useful in that it helps with knowing what they are likely to want from you.

Overall, understanding precisely *who your customers really are* is (of course) a vitally important process, but it's just as important to understand *what your customers are really getting from you,* so let's look at this now.

Understanding what your customers are really getting from you

Mark McCormack's *What They Don't Teach You at Harvard Business School,* contains many great anecdotes. One of the best concerns a conversation McCormack once had with one of his clients, André Heiniger, then the chairman of Rolex.

McCormack relates that he once asked Heiniger how things were in the watch business.

'I really haven't the faintest idea,' Heiniger replied.

McCormack, astonished that the chairman of one of the most famous watch manufacturers in the world could possibly respond like this, asked Heiniger what he meant.

'Rolex is not *in* the watch business,' Heiniger said. 'Rolex is in the *luxury* business.'

This anecdote says, in essence, everything we ought to bear in mind when we think of the enormously important matter of understanding what our customers are getting from us.

Notice, by the way, that the sub-title of this section is 'The importance of understanding what your customers are really getting from you' rather than 'the importance of understanding what you are really supplying to your customers'.

The distinction is essential, because what really matters is, indeed, what *your customers* are getting from *you.*

Focusing on what you are supplying to your customers is less important and may even be unhelpful. After all, a new recruit at Rolex, who does not yet understand the business, might well think that Rolex is supplying its customers with watches (which is obviously true at one level), without understanding yet that what the customers are actually getting from it are, above all, luxuries.

As a matter of common sense, you can only hope to keep your customers happy if you properly understand what they are getting from you.

I'm not saying that if you do understand this, that means that your customers *are* getting what they want from you – of course this won't necessarily be the case. But certainly, your only useful starting-point in managing your relationships with your customers is knowing what they are getting from you right now.

You don't need to be heading a major global brand like Rolex to be obliged to do some hard thinking and research when working out what your customers are really getting from you. Most businesses have constraints on their understanding of what their customers are getting from them, and some businesses get it wrong completely.

For instance, take typewriter companies in the years before the 1980s, when word-processors began to make a dent in the market for typewriters before taking over the market completely.

During the late nineteenth century, and for much of the twentieth century until the 1980s, typewriter manufacture was big business. Yet the only typewriter manufacturer who survived to be big in selling word-processors was IBM, the manufacturer of the famous 'golfball' typewriter (which used a golfball-shaped printing head that moved too fast for the eye to see). IBM was a special case, as it only made typewriters as a sideline; its original business had been making punched-card electromechanical 'tabulator' business machines that were the world's first automatic data processing devices and, incidentally, the direct ancestor of the first electromechanical digital computer, funded by IBM and completed in 1944.

Most organisations that specialised in selling typewriters failed to make the transition to word-processors because these organisations had not fully grasped what they were selling. They thought they were selling typewriters, but in fact, what they were selling *were machines that allowed customers to create, produce and print out documents.*

If the typewriter manufacturers had understood this, they would have jumped at the chance to sell word-processors, which of course offer the fantastic advantage of making it far easier to create successive iterations of documents: and trust me, anyone writing a book knows how important *that* is. You need a good word-processor *and* a large waste-paper basket. And I bet that's true of J.K. Rowling, too.

Ultimately, there's no shortcut to knowing what the real meaning is to your customers of what they are getting from you. Practical research aimed at finding out what customers think of the products and services they get from you, and the role these products and services play in their lives, is essential.

However, applying sheer common sense and your knowledge of human psychology and behaviour to the matter is also important.

Applying this type of thinking to various types of products and services can reveal some interesting, and even surprising, conclusions. We have already mentioned luxury watches, and that André Heiniger of Rolex knew that Rolex was in the luxury business rather than the watch business. Let's now look at a few more examples of products and services where the real nature of what customers are getting from the product or service is by no means as straightforward as one might, at first, imagine.

Diet books

These are, of course (at least on the face of it) designed to help us lose weight. But the inescapable fact is that – judging from the very high sales figures of the most successful of these books – there are millions more people buying such books than actually *losing* weight. This suggests that what customers are getting from the books is very different from mere dietary advice.

It appears that what readers really get from buying a diet book is *the feeling of gratification that they are doing something positive about losing weight*. Indeed, this must be so, as only a small proportion of readers actually go ahead and put the advice into action and lose weight.

The problem is that losing weight is hard; it involves depriving oneself to some extent – or if you want to lose a lot of weight, to a great extent – of the pleasure of eating and it involves getting hungry. Being hungry will make you feel unhappy to start with, though after a while your stomach shrinks and you don't need so much food and you eat less anyway and you don't feel hungry any more.

All the same, dieting is hard. Buying a diet book is a pleasant way to feel you are making progress with this aim without having to suffer.

Lottery tickets

Obviously, people buy a lottery ticket because they want to win the lottery. But as the vast majority of people don't achieve this aim, and will in fact not *expect* to win, common sense suggests that what customers really get from buying a lottery ticket is *the feeling of hope that they might win.* Buyers of lottery tickets can enjoy this feeling between buying the ticket and the results of the draw being publicised. What they are therefore really buying is a *psychological gratification.* Though in fact this shouldn't surprise us, because in fact, if you delve into what customers are getting from many things they're buying, you realise that what they are actually buying *is* usually, above all, again some psychological benefit.

What people who hope to win the lottery don't usually think about is that the same statistical forces that make it, on balance, fantastically *un*likely that they will win the lottery are also protecting them from statistically unlikely *negative* events such as being struck by lightning, having a tree falling on them, suddenly dying from a rare disease, and so on.

This point helps to emphasise the essential unreality of the hope that you will win the lottery when you buy a ticket: the hope is strong enough to prompt the purchase of a ticket but in practice all the customer is really likely to get from the transaction *is* hope.

The statistical facts speak for themselves. In the UK lottery, where the chance of winning the Match Six jackpot (i.e. your ticket matches the winning selection of all six numbers from 49 possibilities) is more than 13 million to one, if you bought five lottery tickets per week you would, on average, have to play the game for more than 51,000 years before you could expect to win the jackpot. Not even Methuselah lived *that* long.

Also, because the Match Six jackpot payout is actually usually a lot less than the c£13,000,000 it should be (the really big payouts only come when there is a 'rollover' of an unwon jackpot from one draw or more than one draw to another), and because the jackpot is often shared, even if you were able to purchase all 13 million sets of numbers (in practice, no facilities for making multiple purchases exist) and so could guarantee yourself at least the Match Six jackpot win and many subsidiary prizes, you would still almost certainly make a substantial loss.

Luxury watches

We have already seen what the chairman of Rolex thought was the true nature of the business he was in.

But there is more to say about luxury watches, because as all mobile phones today have the time on them, there is really no need for people to buy watches *at all* if they carry a mobile phone.

I don't know what the proportion is, globally, of owners of luxury watches who also have mobile phones, but no doubt it is very high, and presumably above 95 percent.

The watches are clearly being bought for some other reason than to tell the time; it's not even that the owners don't have a need for luxury watch; they most likely don't even have a need for a watch at all. The purchase is simply another psychological gratification.

Which is, by the by, a perfectly good reason for buying it. We spend much of our lives seeking to feel good about ourselves. As this is by no means always an easy task; if purchasing a luxury watch (and so providing employment to the people who design and make the luxury watch) is a short-cut to some psychological gratification, fair enough.

Holidays

One could very reasonably say that a customer gets two benefits from buying a holiday. The first is the enjoyment of the holiday, the second is the enjoyment of the memory of the holiday.

The science-fiction writer, Philip K. Dick, in his short story 'We can remember it for you wholesale', postulates an organisation that is able to 'sell' a memory of specific experiences to its customers. This short story was used as the basis for the ingenious but somewhat gratuitously violent Arnold Schwarzenegger movie *Total Recall* (1990).

The memory of a holiday will almost always last longer than the holiday itself. If implanting the memory of an experience ever became technically feasible (which presumably it will at some point, as memory is either stored chemically or electrically, and with the right method both could surely be manipulated) holidays would, at one level, become unnecessary. Memories of a holiday could indeed just be implanted. Busy, time-poor executives might even regard this as a better way of 'having' a holiday than actually spending a week idling on a beach or sipping red wine on the terrace of a French château.

Who knows – perhaps, after memory implantation becomes feasible – actually *going* on holiday will be seen a low-status activity only practised by those insufficiently busy to prefer the high-status, quick and easy, memory implantation alternative!

Drugs (i.e. drugs sold legally on prescription)

What customers get from drugs consists, like holidays, of a two-part benefit.

Firstly, there are the therapeutic benefits that are measurable by an appropriate analytical technique.

Secondly, there are – again – the psychological benefits of taking the drug. I doubt whether any doctor would deny that these psychological benefits play some part in assisting to drive home the measurable therapeutic benefits.

This is especially so, as the 'placebo effect' in drug-taking is a well-known and entirely respected fact of medical practice, rather than a kind of medical form of astrology, as you might at first thought expect it to be. The use of placebos is essential in testing drugs in order to identify therapeutic benefits. In all tests involving placebos, a significant number of patients, who have only taken the placebos, report definite therapeutic benefits.

Television

What people really get from TV goes well beyond the benefit (if any) of the actual programmes. Many people, for example, watch TV to relax after a hard day's work, with the implication that they might actually prefer to watch programmes that are not too mentally demanding. (The nature of many TV programmes today being what it is, this is hardly a requirement that is likely to be frustrated.)

Families often watch TV together just to *be* together; one often senses that what they watch is secondary to this.

People living alone may watch TV to gain a sense of companionship, illusory though it is likely to be.

Original Listerine mouthwash

This mouthwash tastes unpleasant and is so strong that if you hold some in your mouth for more than a few seconds is starts to burn the inside of your mouth. Yet the feeling of freshness one has in one's mouth after using it is popular with many people, especially as original Listerine mouthwash contains active ingredients that are known to combat plaque and gum disease.

One could successfully argue that the very fact that original Listerine mouthwash has such a strong taste is one of the benefits its customers see it as conferring on them.

Indeed, in the United States, the first television advertisements for Listerine – featuring a young Morgan Freeman – had that actor playing a telephone cable engineer who, from a vantage point on a telegraph pole, praised the effectiveness of Listerine, saying that if it didn't taste so strong, he figured 'it wouldn't be doing such a good job.'

I've no idea why the ad depicted someone who repaired telephone cables as likely to be in particular need of Listerine.

Energy drinks

At a medical level, 'energy' drinks are completely unnecessary for anyone having a healthy and balanced diet. Even if someone does want a sudden rush of caffeine and sugar, a cup of hot sweetened coffee or of hot chocolate will generally achieve this objective better than a can of a cold fizzy drink.

But this simple logical point does not interest purchasers of energy drinks, who get a whole range of psychological benefits from the purchase that would be lost on people who are not fans of these drinks, much as the pleasure of listening to 'rap' music is lost on those who are not fans of this kind of music.

These benefits, which lovers of energy drinks perceive themselves as enjoying when they buy their favourite drink, arise from factors relating to status, lifestyle choice and peer pressure. The benefits have made energy drinks a global sales phenomenon in recent years.

The most successful energy drink of all, Red Bull, sells about three million cans a day globally. The fact that it tastes like sweetened mouthwash without having any pretensions to offering even the benefits that mouthwash offers, doesn't seem to put its fans off. There is, after all, no accounting for taste, though Red Bull's accountants presumably don't agree.

Insurance

This is a useful, and relatively rare, example of a product where the prime benefit is psychological.

After all, in most cases, when people buy insurance, they actively *don't want* the event against which they are insuring to happen.

The benefit they get from the insurance policy is the peace of mind that, should the undesired event happen, they will receive certain benefits from the policy that will help to offset the impact of the event, but the benefits are unlikely ever to be seen as offering a *complete* offsetting of the undesirable event.

Two vital conclusions

This brief consideration of what customers are really getting from some examples of products and services offers two particularly useful conclusions for our analysis of the nature of the customer relationship.

Firstly, psychological gratification is in fact the prime benefit of many products and services. It follows that the more the organisation knows about these psychological gratifications, the more likely it is to be successful in selling its products and services to customers.

Secondly, most organisations selling specific products and services to customers probably most likely have more extensive opportunities than they might imagine to embody — in their marketing and advertising activity — their knowledge of what their customers really get from their products and services.

Ways of developing, understanding and making use of insights into the emotional satisfactions that consumers enjoy from a product or service

Once an organisation understands what its customers truly get from it, the organisation can indeed take steps to embody that knowledge, often very successfully, in marketing and advertising.

Of course, many organisations already do this successfully, though there is always more that can be done, the more one knows about customers. The canniest organisations undertake quality thinking and customer research *before* a new product is launched, in order to take every step to maximise the success of its launch.

The market research industry — and especially those market research agencies that mainly concern themselves with what are known as fast-moving consumer goods (fmcg), which tend to be the brands you buy from supermarkets — conducts extensive research, and makes detailed recommendations based on the research, to help brandowners who want to market new products and also who want to refine ways of selling and marketing products that are already on the market.

For example, a UK-based market research agency, MMR Research Worldwide, is a pioneer in researching the emotional appeal to customers of the *sensory signatures* of products. The importance of this work is reflected in the organisation's considerable success in the UK, its work throughout the world, and its opening of overseas offices, including in the United States and China.

David Thomson, founder and chairman MMR Research Worldwide, has been a consumer psychologist since the 1970s. He also holds the honorary title of Visiting Professor in the Department of Food and Nutritional Sciences at the University of Reading. I am grateful to Professor Thomson for the following thinking on sensory signatures, thinking in which he is a world pioneer.

Sensory signatures are some aspect of a product or service that bring pleasure via one or more of our senses. For example, if you like freshly-roasted chicken, the sight and smell of the chicken just out of the oven will be complemented by the sizzle of the pan juices in the baking-tray and the anticipated taste. There may even be a touch sensation too if you take the hot, rather greasy, drumstick in your hand when you eat from it.

Commercial food and drink brands provide sensory pleasure too, often in a very consciously – though by no means necessarily *cynically* – engineered way. The taste and smell of a particular food or drink brand will be complemented by the sight of its familiar package. Touch may be involved too, such as (say) in the cool, smooth feel of a particular chocolate bar. As for the sense of hearing, it's true that this is less often involved with food or drink brands than with the other senses, but this is not to say that it is never a factor. An example would be the 'snap, crackle and pop' of Rice Krispies when milk is poured over them.

The precise impact of a sensory signature will depend on:

- its fundamental nature
- its quality
- its duration
- its magnitude
- the extent to which it is liked
- the manner in which it is *conceptualised*

This notion of *conceptualisation* is vital in how Professor Thomson sees sensory signatures. His thinking on this matter requires its own terminology, and in his way of looking at sensory signatures he draws a clear distinction between:

- what a sensory signature *is* – which he calls *perception*
- what a sensory signature *means* – which he calls *conceptualisation*

Understanding precisely what a sensory signature means to individual consumers is something that Professor Thomson's organisation investigates in its research.

Essentially the crucial point is this: a particular sensory signature will not only bring pleasure via one or more senses but will also produce some degree of emotional satisfaction. This emotional satisfaction will not be produced on every consumer, but if emotional satisfaction is produced on enough consumers in the sense that it is possible through research to gain some understanding and analysis of the nature of the emotional satisfaction in question, that emotional satisfaction will, clearly, be of great importance in how a particular product is marketed.

In Professor Thomson's terminology, emotional satisfaction is a result of how a particular perception is conceptualised, given that we are using the word 'perception' here in the specialised meaning of what a particular sensory signature is.

For example, consider the well-known brand of yeast extract Marmite. Its taste is, in Professor Thomson's terminology, a perception that leads to a conceptualisation which will in turn result in emotional satisfaction. For example, some consumers may find that they conceptualise the taste of Marmite in a way that brings them the emotional satisfaction of thinking of their childhoods and comfortable, snug tea-times with their brother and sisters in the company of their mother. If research were to show that this is a sufficiently widespread source of emotional satisfaction resulting from the taste of Marmite, an effort may be made to promote this comfortable childhood association in advertising and marketing.

Ideally, a brandowner prefers that a particular emotional satisfaction resulting from a particular sensory signature will:

- be associated only with that one brand
- be something consumers like and want to experience repeatedly, and so they buy the brand again and again.

When the appeal of a sensory signature has been established among consumers, brandowners quite rightly try hard to ensure the standardisation of the brand in order to ensure that customers enjoy the same gratification every time they buy the brand. There is always the risk that if the brandowner changes the nature of the product or service, even to what may seem like a minimal extent, the sensory signature may no longer be delivered and customers will cease to be loyal to the brand.

The classic example of a disaster in this respect occurred in April 1985, when the Coca-Cola Company, amidst much publicity, changed the formula for Coca-Cola to give the drink a new flavour, consequently a new sensory signature and crucially a new conceptual profile. Even if the new flavour had been liked more, the change in conceptual profile would have detracted hugely from the total experience of drinking Coke and led to a reduced emotional satisfaction of drinking Coke.

Perhaps for this very reason, the new flavour, New Coke, was disastrously unpopular with customers, and in the face of global complaints from customers, Coca-Cola within a few months re-launched the old, familiar, much loved drink and called it 'Classic Cola'. This is now again by far the most popular version of the drink. New Coke was discontinued as a major product by Coca-Cola, though it is still produced by some semi-independent bottlers and is popular in some niche markets, including, reportedly, the United States territory of Samoa. So if you like New Coke, you can go to Samoa and enjoy it.

This example of a drink manufacturer getting it wrong is a dramatic illustration of what we might, in any case, imagine, which is that food and drink brands lend themselves with particular ease to having sensory signatures built into them, simply because our senses of taste and smell are closely bound up with our strongest sensuous pleasures. However, sensory signatures can, as we've seen, apply to any of our senses.

An example of a non-food sensory signature that relates to hearing is the quiet purr of the Rolls-Royce's engine one hears when one is inside the car. In the past, this sensory signature featured heavily in advertisements for Rolls-Royce cars, largely at the suggestions of advertising guru David Ogilvy, whose organisation handled the advertising for Rolls-Royce. Ogilvy was a great believer in adverts communicating interesting information about products and services.

Many sensory signatures are visual. The bright scarlet colour of a can of Coca-Cola and the purple of a Cadbury's chocolate wrapper are just two examples of successful sensory signatures that, like all the best ones, are capable of wooing customers over several decades.

As **Professor Thomson** explains:

Today, new ways of understanding how consumers feel about brands are giving brandowners unprecedented insight into what's happening at an emotional level when consumers make buying decisions. Armed with this knowledge, brandowners have exciting opportunities to engineer emotions into their brands and enjoy global success.

Up until now, many brandowners haven't always appreciated that when packaged goods are being sold to consumers, the product itself – not only the branding, packaging or manner in which the product is promoted – has an inherent emotional impact on the people who buy it. This explains why so many product launches and relaunches fail.

Instead of focusing on these vitally important emotional factors, too many brandowners ask their market research teams simply to investigate liking and propensity-to-buy. But in truth neither is an effective predictor of whether consumers are going to buy a product, let alone an indication of whether they'll make it part of their regular weekly shopping.

The fact is, consumers like a lot of things they don't buy and buy a lot of things they don't like. This suggests that consumer behaviour is being guided by factors other than mere liking. But if that's so, what factors are consumers really being influenced by and how can we measure these factors?

Having laid out the groundwork of his philosophy of why consumers buy what they buy, Professor Thomson expands on it. In what he writes below he elaborates on his approach to perception and conceptualisation: concepts I have already outlined above in order to introduce how he sees them.

> *My own thinking on consumer psychology is that traditional market research tests, which try to investigate liking and propensity to buy, fail to capture an adequate overview of the real reasons why consumers buy things.*
>
> *The reason for this, in my view, is that it is all very well knowing whether or not someone likes something, but mere liking may not be enough for someone actually to part with their money to buy it, because they lack the motivation and desire to do so.*

This point ties in with my own remarks, earlier in this chapter, about the difference between liking and wanting.

Professor Thomson proceeds:

> *Instead, I believe that people buy things for the same reasons they do other things in their lives: **because they get a reward**. We can call this reward positivity.*
>
> *I also think it's important to identify the experience of heightened positivity, which can be referred to as a 'spike' of positivity. Heightened positivity may come about as a result of special events in our lives such as holidays, falling in love, getting married, and also as a consequence of more day-to-day events: a good lunch or an excellent cup of coffee, for example.*
>
> *In practice, most of the time people are usually content to enjoy a stream of little spikes of positivity from their lives. Indeed, it's very likely this is the way evolution has designed us to enjoy life.*
>
> *Many spikes of positivity are, of course, unrelated to the choice of a branded product or service, yet brandowners should take every reasonable step to ensure that their brand becomes intimately associated with spikes of positivity wherever possible.*

*Doing this makes hard commercial sense. Consumers will stop buying a brand if, for some reason, it ceases bringing positivity into their lives. But brandowners should not only be defensive. They need to know exactly **what** their brand means to consumers and **why** their brand means what it does.*

*Yes, it's true that brandowners have for a long time set their brands in a promotional context which communicates the positivity that using the brand will bring. Car adverts, for example, don't just show a shiny new car in the showroom; the ad will typically depict the car in some picturesque or exotic location unlikely to bear much resemblance to the M25 on a wet and dark Friday evening. Or Gillette razors, for instance, are advertised by showing a male model enjoying a particularly close and wonderful shave, and Gillette's ambitious strapline, **the best a man can get,** is obviously designed to make you forget that the razors are simply ingeniously engineered small pieces of metal and plastic.*

*But even though brandowners have often had an intuitive sense of the need to promote their brand in a context of positivity, they can now use exactly the same principle as a basis for a more structured approach towards **all** their marketing activity.*

*In particular, what should their market research really be doing? Nothing less than helping brandowners identify and optimise the **triggers** that give consumers a heightened sense of positivity through their emotional experience of the brand.*

By focusing specifically on emotional factors a brandowner can create a compelling point of difference versus competitors.

What exactly are these triggers?

*This brings us to the vital matter of the product's **sensory characteristics**.*

*Most, if not all, of what we experience when we interact with an object in the physical world is channelled to the mind via our senses. Brandowners need to engineer deliberately-crafted associations — **sensory signatures** — between sensory characteristics and brand identity into their brand. Brandowners* can do this by taking advantage of their emotional understanding of how consumers see the brand.

Red Bull is a successful example of this. Even people who love Red Bull would probably agree that it is not one of the most pleasant-tasting soft drinks, yet its unusual and quirky taste has successfully distinguished it from other carbonates which often have adolescent or juvenile connotations.

We can call the process of experiencing the sensory characteristics of different stimuli **perception**. Yet perception is only part of the story, because what matters most of all, and what in fact amounts to a key for unlocking the mystery of consumer choice, is **the meaning consumers attach in their minds to the sensory signatures they perceive.**

This process of attaching meaning to perception can be referred to as **conceptualisation**. Conceptualisation matters precisely because buying behaviours **don't** only arise from perception but also from how we conceptualise what we perceive. In other words, **we make a buying choice because of what the sensory signatures mean to us.**

How does conceptualisation work in practice? In the case of Red Bull, the drink's edginess, associations with extreme sports and its promise to 'vitalise body and mind' and 'give you wings', is adult and aspirational. The associated functional, emotional and other more abstract conceptualisations created by Red Bull's branding are then delivered by the drink. This is achieved in part via the physiologically and psychologically active compounds in the liquid but also via the associations that have developed between the drink's distinctive sensory characteristics and consumers' conceptualisations of the brand.

Any competent drinks company could copy the Red Bull liquid in most respects. However, the associations that have developed between the brand-generated conceptualisations and the drink's sensory characteristics are uniquely owned by Red Bull and no other brand. 'Me too' energy drink brands do not enjoy the enormous customer mandate that Red Bull enjoys.

The importance of conceptualisation in consumer choice is very great. Armed with an understanding of it, brandowners can create market research programmes designed to give them a detailed understanding of precisely what kind of emotional meanings consumers attach to their products through conceptualisation.

At MMR Research Worldwide, our philosophy of branding is based around a matrix that plots three aspects of a brand – **branding** (we take this to mean how a brandowner communicates, promotes and advertises their branded offer), **product** and **packaging** – against the three criteria of how the whole branded offer is conceptualised by consumers. The three criteria are:

- **Liking:** this refers to the immediate enjoyment caused by the product experience.
- **Emotionality:** this refers to the emotional conceptualisations being conveyed.
- **Functionality:** this refers to the functional conceptualisations that are being conveyed. For example, does a new energy drink **taste like** it will keep you awake with the ability to dance all night? This might well be different from the **actual**, scientifically provable power the drink has to give energy to its customers.

Applying market research to the task of investigating what a brand means emotionally to consumers brings scientifically sound, quantitative research to an area often dominated by qualitative research. Brandowners can now use these research techniques to get access to brand and product profiles that reveal all the associated emotions and conceptualisations – putting a measure on every one.

For a brandowner, the secret of success is to make the product a response to what the research has uncovered, and to optimise all elements of the branded offer (such as the formulation or product design, packaging, marketing and promotion) so that they are conceptually harmonious in order to maximise their potential emotional appeal to consumers, whenever and wherever they encounter the brand.

Professor Thomson's fascinating and in-depth thinking in essence aims to exploit – and not in any cynical fashion, either – a particular aspect of human psychology for the purposes of making consumer products not only attractive to customers but – and this is I think a major point – part of customers' own emotional experience and enjoyment of life.

Who is to say that doing this is not an important service to humanity? Who is to say that a teenager may not get as much of a buzz from drinking Red Bull with his or her friends as an opera buff gets from watching a great performance of *Madame Butterfly*? As apostles of customer-centricity, it is not our job to make judgements about what people want. Instead, our job is to find out *what* they want and, if our business involves meeting that need, to meet it to the very best of our abilities.

When we look at Professor Thomson's philosophy of customer desire, we can see, I think, that his approach is an extrapolation of the basic principle that *organisations need to take every step to understand what their customers are really getting from them.*

You don't, by the way, need to be working within an organisation supplying some product or service on a profit-making basis to need to have a real understanding of your customers are getting from you. Acquiring this understanding is also, in fact, essential in the public sector. Sue Redmond, corporate director of community services at Charteris client Wiltshire Council, oversees a team of almost to 1,500 council employees. As Sue told me:

> It's vitally important that we at Wiltshire Council know precisely what our customers – which is how we nowadays prefer to refer to the users of our services – are getting from us. We don't see ourselves as just supplying services. Instead, we see ourselves as helping to make their lives better.

This thinking was behind Wiltshire Council's successful initiative to effect a comprehensive restructuring of its community care department based *not* around different types of service being administered and delivered from separate 'silos', but instead based around the needs of the customers.

One of many results of the restructuring was that customers phoning into Wiltshire Council who have needs that impinge on different areas of the council's community care operations are no longer passed from one department to another. Instead, the council employee who takes the call is trained to, and has the resources to, handle *all* the customer's needs from one phone call.

The big secret at the heart of this book

Everything I've said so far can, in a way, be said to dovetail into the big secret at the heart of this book.

The big secret is this: if your great aim is that the customers in all the different areas of your life actively want what you're offering them (and, if they're commercial customers, are willing to buy it from you), you must find within yourself the energy, discipline and imagination to see the world from your customers' point of view and then (most likely) adjust your behaviour towards your customers, and the nature of what you're offering them, accordingly.

That's it. That really is the big secret.

On the face of it, the secret's straightforward enough.

Putting it into practice, however, require energy, discipline, imagination... and hard work.

Above all, putting the big secret into practice requires you to want to see things from your customers' point of view.

Personally, I believe that the reason why developing an ability to want to do this is difficult is that we are programmed by evolution to care mostly about our own agenda and that of our immediate family. Caring about the agenda of people apart from ourselves and our immediate family is, I think, in a sense unnatural, at least as far as evolution is concerned.

But, as the newspaper columnist Christina Patterson has pointed out in *The Independent* newspaper:

> *A society can't function, or at least it can't function very well, without the realisation that people outside your family are as real as the people in it. There has, in recent years, been a*

growing emphasis on the 'hard-working family' as the seat of all that's good: parents battling for their darlings' rights and now, God help us, even clubbing together to start schools. There's a name for a community that puts family first. It's called the Mafia.

The realisation that, as Christina Patterson puts it, *people outside your family are as real as the people in it*, is one of the most important realisations I am urging in this book.

Why is the big secret of customer-centricity so rarely put into practice? Moreover, even if you are keen to put it into practice, why can it seem so hard to do so?

The reason, I think, is indeed this: *evolution did not programme us to be customer-centric.*

Yet just as evolution did not programme us to fly from one country to another, or indeed to fly at all, or to climb Mount Everest, or to dive deep below the surface of the sea, with hard training and the right equipment we can do these and other non-evolution-programmed things. The main requirement, however, is that we *want* to do these things.

All this also applies to being customer-centric.

Dale Carnegie's world-famous self-help book *How To Win Friends and Influence People*, first published in 1936, contains several excellent anecdotes supporting his aim of urging readers to win success by thinking of the needs and agenda of others, rather than of themselves. The need to do this is arguably the most important theme of Carnegie's book.

In one of the many excellent and instructive anecdotes the book contains, Dale Carnegie observes that while he himself is very fond of strawberries and cream, when he goes fishing he doesn't put strawberries and cream on the hook but rather a worm or a grasshopper.

This is an excellent point: in this situation the fish he is hoping to catch are in effect his customers and so putting a worm or grasshopper on the hook is a clear and direct homage to their agenda.

So am I suggesting that the entire strategy and art of what I'm urging here in *The Customer-Centric You* – and very frequently implementing it *is* an art as much as a strategy – can be boiled down to the commonsense point that if you go fishing, you need to bait the hook with what the fish likes to eat rather than what *you* like to eat?

Well, no, not completely. The fishing anecdote is powerful, and very much worth including here, because it illustrates the need to keep the agenda of others in mind at all times.

However, one factor seriously limits the effectiveness of the anecdote.

The limiting factor is the *cynicism* with which an angler baits the hook. The angler doesn't truly care about the fish's agenda – especially not if the angler is fishing for the pot rather than practising catch-and-release!

The angler baits the hook with a fundamentally selfish intent, but if you want to be all you can be to all the customers in your life, you need to consider *their* agenda with sincerity and genuine empathy, not with cynicism.

A cynical response to customers will not get you far, because if you don't want to know your customers properly, and if you don't want to care about their agenda, there will inevitably be a limit on how well you ever *will* know your customers.

We can, indeed, even extend this analogy to angling itself.

The truth is that worms are not necessarily good baits for all kinds of fish. Depending on the water you're fishing and the type of fish you're aiming to catch, baits such as sweetcorn, luncheon meat, parboiled potatoes and 'boilies' (an artificial bait made from egg protein and flavourings) are likely to be more effective, especially when you're fishing for the dream fish of most freshwater anglers: the carp. Or I should say, *the dream fish of most freshwater anglers in the UK and much of Europe.* In the United States, the carp is inexplicably regarded as something of a pest.

If you want to catch truly worthwhile fish, you need to be sensitive to, and aware of, the precise kind of baits most likely to tempt these fish to bite.

Moreover, a true angler does not fish for freshwater fish for the pot, but puts the fish back after catching them so that the fish can grow bigger and can, maybe, be caught again.

Maybe you can see an analogy with customers here?

In *How To Win Friends and Influence People*, Dale Carnegie quotes the Viennese psychologist Alfred Adler, who in his book *What Life Should Mean To You*, says:

> *It is the individual who is not interested in his fellow men who has the greatest difficulties in life and provides the greatest injury to others. It is from among such individuals that all human failures spring.*

In Chapter 15 of her novel *Middlemarch* (1871), the English author George Eliot offers an intriguing analysis of human ambition and why it so often doesn't usually get fulfilled.

Firstly, she sets down her belief that most people (she refers to men, but it applies to women just as much), who may have once wanted to really make something of their lives, fail to do so.

> *... in the multitude of middle-aged men who go about their vocations in a daily course determined for them much in the same way as the tie of their cravats, there is always a good number who once meant to shape their own deeds and alter the world a little.*

George Eliot's precise analysis of the reason why most people fail 'to shape their own deeds and alter the world a little' is rather obscure; it is difficult not to feel that she suffers here from not having access to modern psychological terms. But the nub of what she is saying is clear enough. This is that what spoils the chances for most people of fulfilling their ambitions are what George Eliot describes as 'spots of commonness' in their minds and personalities that, in effect, reduce the quality of their performance.

By 'spots of commonness' she is not making any reference to social class. Instead, she means negative aspects to their personality and to their thinking, with these negative factors conspiring to introduce a level of mediocrity to their minds and, by extension, to what they think, do and say.

I profoundly believe that, for most people, a major cause of 'spots of commonness' in their personality and thinking – and consequently a principal reason why they fail to achieve all they want to achieve, or could achieve, in their careers — is a lack of ability, or desire, to empathise with their agenda of others.

On that note, and with our preliminary discussion complete, let's now turn to the notion of customer-centricity.

Defining customer-centricity

Here's a good, working definition of the core concept at the heart of this book:

> *Customer-centricity is an attribute of any entity that is doing all that it can reasonably do to focus on, and minister to, the agenda of its customers.*

This entity can be anything: a privately owned, for-profit organisation; a publicly owned, for-profit organisation; or a public sector organisation such as a local or regional authority or any central government organisation.

The entity can also be an individual.

When an individual fully exhibits the attribution of customer-centricity, that person could be said to be fully customer-centric: *the customer-centric you*.

Being customer-centric does not, of course, mean that *all* the organisation or the person does is focus on the customer, but the fact remains that the matter of being truly customer-centric will be a major factor in how the organisation operates, or how the organisation thinks.

At Charteris, the business and information technology consultancy where I head the business consulting practice, we define customer-centricity in somewhat more formal terms, and with the emphasis on seeing customer-centricity as the result of a transformational process. However, the upshot of the definition is the same.

Charteris's definition of customer-centricity is:

> *the process of ensuring that every individual and department within an organisation is taking every step feasible to add value to what the organisation does for its customers.*

In thinking about and responding to the needs of customers, customer-centricity is the ideal state for which to aim. An organisation that truly exhibits customer-centricity can hardly fail but be successful, and individuals who are truly customer-centric in their attitude to all the customers in their lives, are likely to be having the *time* of their lives.

Why? Because truly customer-centric people are being all they can be at work and at play, and other people in both spheres are likely to love them.

Essentially, customer-centricity – the strategic business discipline which this book is all about, is just a way for implementing, in any organisational structure, a reliable and effective mechanism for putting the Big Secret into action.

And it follows that if you are to become *the customer-centric you*, you need to become someone who, reliably and effectively, *puts the Big Secret in action in your own life.*

Yes. If we are to become truly customer-centric in our thinking, the need to understand and sincerely care about our customers' agenda must become, in effect, our religion.

We should also remember that, while it's useful, at a practical level, to think of an organisation as being customer-centric, in practice it is not the organisation that is customer-centric, but rather it is the attitude and outlook of the people who work for an organisation who will decide whether the organisation is customer-centric or not.

And this is the point, and ultimately the reason why *The Customer-Centric You* focuses firstly on people and only secondly on organisations. Personal, individual customer-centricity is, ultimately, what matters in your professional life just as it is what matters in your personal life.

And – again – if you're serious about being customer-centric you can't possibly separate your 'professional persona' from your 'personal life persona'.

The simple fact and undeniable truth is this: **if you want to become the customer-centric you, you need to embrace customer-centricity as a holistic attribute of your entire personality.**

2

A HISTORICAL PERSPECTIVE ON CUSTOMER-CENTRICITY

The need for customer-centricity isn't something that has only surfaced recently. It has existed for as long as humans have provided one another with things they need in exchange for things they can supply. We can't really understand customer-centricity properly unless we start by looking at how today's customer-centric requirements have evolved from the past.

The earliest times

I believe we can assert with confidence that it is only since about the year 1750 AD – at the start of the period which lasted for about a century and which historians today call the Industrial Revolution – that customer-centricity in professional life has been a major practical challenge.

Customer-centricity in private life was, doubtless, a challenge ever since our species *homo sapiens* first began to evolve from the previous species, *homo habilis*, about 1.5 million years ago. But even this personal kind of customer-centric challenge would have been less pressing before the onset of industrialisation in the mid eighteenth century, when most people lived in small village communities, or within small communities in towns, and would have had their circle of acquaintances limited in most cases to less than a hundred people.

The precise time by when the modern form of *homo sapiens* to which we belong had evolved is a matter of some conjecture among anthropologists, but it's most likely that the modern form of our species had evolved by 100,000 years ago. That means that for those 100,000 years people have had the same intellectual and physical abilities as people do today.

The years since 1750 AD have consequently been only a tiny part of the story of modern humankind, though the years since then have also seen developments in the evolution of human societies and communities that have transformed the world beyond anything that could be imagined before then.

Even William Shakespeare, the greatest and most imaginative writer who has ever lived, gives not the slightest indication anywhere in his work of anticipating the future world of giant cities, rapid international air travel, and global communications networks, that have made life in the twenty-first century surely seem, in many respects, like life on another planet compared with that of any century in the past.

For most of the history of modern man, until about 6,000 years ago, the vast majority of people dwelled in small communities that survived – depending on their geographical location and their stage of cultural evolution – by hunting, gathering and agriculture. There were some towns and cities, and possibly also some towns and cities existed during prehistoric times that have left little or no traces behind for archaeologists to find.

But generally the existence of significant prehistoric towns is the stuff of fantasy rather than reality. Towns and cities started to evolve about 6,000 years ago, at about the same time as the evolution of a vitally important cultural skill – writing – that allowed information to be handed down readily from one generation to another.

Life in towns and cities needed complex organisation and management. It's no coincidence that writing was invented at about the same time as towns and cities started to proliferate.

In particular, it was especially important, in new and more complex communities where people did not all know one another, that *precise* and *durable* records could be kept of ownership of assets.

There is considerable evidence that writing evolved from the use of clay tokens, stored in clay containers, with the tokens standing for some asset such as a house or an animal. Because the clay tokens were not visible inside the containers, it was convenient to make marks on the side of the container to show what tokens were inside the container. Obviously, once the system used for making the marks became standardised and also started to carry enough authority, the tokens themselves became unnecessary, as the marks themselves would have been enough. One way of making marks was to draw a quick diagram of what was owned, and it is indeed, for instance fact that our letter 'A' has evolved, via the alphabet of ancient Semitic peoples, and via that of the Phoenicians, the Greeks and the Romans, from a drawing of a cow's head.

With the invention of writing, which allowed events in a particular community to be recorded as ownership to be documented, history began. Writing started at different times in different countries; indeed, even today, most languages of the world (including, in fact, most regional dialects of English, do not have a standardised written form).

The first culture that is definitely know to have recorded its history was that of the Sumerians, who first began to flourish about 5,500 years ago, with the Ancient Egyptians first starting to arise as a vigorous culture about 500 years later, at about the same time as the earliest Chinese cultures that recorded their own history.

All these ancient communities developed towns and cities. Economic life, however, remained by modern standards rudimentary, heavily weighted towards agriculture.

The Ancient Egyptian civilisation, for example, was as elaborate and prosperous as it was because the annual inundation of the River Nile flooded the land with rich silt and made Egyptian agriculture highly successful. Many Egyptians became extremely wealthy; the very notion of preserving the body so that it might continue to enjoy a prosperous afterlife derives from the wealth of many Ancient Egyptians.

In these early societies, commercial life was based around buying and selling in marketplaces or among merchants who often travelled surprisingly long distances to buy and sell good. The silk trade, for example, which originated in China – where silk was first produced in around 2700 BC – involved silk fabric and silk thread being transported from China to Europe along a route that can still be traced today.

We can reasonably assume that customer-centricity was not, generally speaking, a major problem in these ancient societies. Market stall holders, traders of all kinds, merchants, artisans, and people (such as surgeons and law-makers) who were offering services we would nowadays regard as professional rather than commercial, would all have their own customers whom they knew personally.

No doubt the particular quality of goods that a seller of products or services had for sale, and how that seller treated existing and new customers, would have determined that person's prosperity. The most important point, though, was that the seller and the customer were known to each other by personal contact, and commercial units remained small.

There are many examples of wealthy families in history. Indeed most countries were run by such families. But such wealth appears in almost all cases to have derived from conquest or some lucky accident, such as possession of land on which valuable raw materials were found, or ownership of extensive tracts of land on which crops were grown. With the possible exception of the Medici family in medieval Italy, there are no great families recorded in history, before the eighteenth century, whose wealth derived substantially from commerce.

Corroborative evidence of the assumption that commerce and industry were mostly small-scale until about 1750 – and this does indeed justify the invention of the term Industrial *Revolution* – is seen in the fact that history has also failed to hand down, from the period prior to the eighteenth century, no examples at all of major commercial or industrial concerns. Even the legendary wealth of Croesus, who was the ruler of Ancient Lydia (modern Turkey) about five centuries before the birth of Christ, derived from agriculture in Ancient Lydia and from that country's maritime trade.

The term 'Industrial Revolution' itself appears to have been the invention of a Frenchman, the diplomat Louis-Guillaume Otto, who on July 6 1799 wrote to a friend in which he claimed that *'une revolution industrielle'* had commenced in his country. What was true of France was even more true at the time of Britain, and in Britain the revolution had begun about half a century earlier.

Our assumption that customer-centricity was not a significant problem before the onset of the Industrial Revolution is, therefore, most likely a sound one. In those days the entire relationship between sellers and customers had an inbuilt mechanism that would ensure customers got properly looked after. If your customers were not happy, there was a real danger that you, and your family, would starve, for these were not societies that had the safety net of a welfare state. Many market stall holders and merchants employed assistants, and certainly these assistants would have been obliged to become, without delay, as customer-focused as their masters if they had wanted to keep their positions.

But generally there is no evidence, until the beginnings of modern industrialised societies during the late eighteenth century, that the relationship between owners of a business and their customers was a significant problem. Business enterprises tended to be small, in most cases involving the members of just one family, and within these small commercial units there would be a vested interest in keeping customers happy.

Even manufacturing was mostly founded on the kind of small manufacturing units – a little factory, for example, staffed by a family and perhaps a few friends – that are still found today, in abundance, in the developing world. It is important, by the way, not to sentimentalise economic units that may too easily seem quaint and picturesque by modern standards: life in them was usually lived on the breadline, and if a customer departed, starvation was always a potential hazard, as, sadly, it so often is in the developing world today.

The first recorded use of the very word 'customer' in English, in the sense, mentioned in Chapter 1, as 'a person who makes a purchase or gives business, especially to any particular seller or establishment', dates from about 1480 AD.

The onset of the Industrial Revolution

The long-established model of economic society based around these commercial or industrial units began to change profoundly in the eighteenth century. The reason for the change was that new types of technological tools were invented that began to be applied to manufacturing. The invention of these tools was both spurred on and complemented by the development of steam power, which freed industry from having to be located near sources of water for powering water-wheels.

The world's first significant application of steam-power and new types of technological tools occurred in the British textiles industry during the eighteenth century. Almost at once, factories grew up that used hundreds of machines, all powered by cords and gearwheels often running from just one large steam-engine. Workers in these factories were often minding the machines and making sure nothing went wrong, rather than operating them manually or with a foot-treadle.

The eighteenth century was a great century for books that expounded practical economic philosophies pointing out the benefits of such economic phenomena as economies of scale and specialisation. In Britain, income tax was often non-existent in the eighteenth century, and only became a permanent part of economic life in the UK (at, initially, a rate of less than three percent per pound earned) during the nineteenth after the passage into law of Sir Robert Peel's Income Tax Act 1842. The law imposed a tax on anyone earning more than £150 per year (a significant sum perhaps about £75,000 today). Entrepreneurs who started successful factories might soon find themselves employing several hundred people and making vast fortunes that were hardly taxed at all.

Richard Arkwright, for example, who pioneered the introduction into the British textiles industry of a machine for increasing the speed of production of spinning yarn, founded a factory in Cromford, Derbyshire in 1771 that was widely regarded at the time as showing how large factories should be run.

Working life at the factory was not for the squeamish. There were two 13-hour shifts – the overlap was designed to avoid any time being wasted between shifts – and any worker who was late was not only deprived of the opportunity to work that day but was docked a day's pay into the bargain. Employment legislation hardly existed; employing people was basically a free-for-all in which employers mostly focused solely on getting the most work from employees for the least pay. Yet it is an indication of just how tough life was for hand-spinners in Arkwright's day that weavers flocked from their little weaving-rooms in their damp cottages to work at Arkwright's mill.

The British Industrial Revolution, and the new society it created and that flourished during the nineteenth century, created an entirely new perspective on customers. The significance of this new perspective was soon recognised by politicians, and by authorities in the area of 'political economy', which was what economics was called in the eighteenth century and for much of the nineteenth.

The British Government, from having in the past mainly existed to manage Britain's defence as well as her overseas conquests, and to deter and punish crime in Britain itself, now found itself in the position of taking an interest in the new industrial and commercial world.

As the renowned economist Adam Smith observed in 1776 in his highly influential book *An Enquiry Into the Nature and Causes of the Wealth of Nations*

> *To found a great empire for the sole purpose of raising up a people of customers, may at first sight appear a project fit only for a nation of shopkeepers. It is, however, a project altogether unfit for a nation of shopkeepers, but extremely fit for a nation whose government is influenced by shopkeepers.*

The significance of this comment lies as much in Smith's recognition of the new importance of the customer as in the sentiment expressed. That said, the comment is inherently an interesting one, and anticipates the gradual trend, during the nineteenth century rather than the eighteenth, for governments to play more of a role in helping to create more efficient environments in which the new kinds of industry and trade could flourish.

Incidentally, the description of Britain as a 'nation of shopkeepers' was first attributed to the American statesman and political philosopher Samuel Adams, who used the phrase during an oration in Philadelphia in 1776. The British retail industry is, in fact, extremely relevant from both a historical and current perspective to the challenge of customer-centricity, but for the moment let's return to the burgeoning industrial scene in Britain of the mid-eighteenth century.

Hundreds or even thousands of people were employed by the largest factories (or 'mills' as they tended to be called in their day, even if they were carrying out activities very different from milling flour or making bread). The vast majority of people working in the mills were indeed involved with minding machines and/or making products that could be sold. These people had little or no contact with customers, who would be dealt with by specialists in the organisation.

Clearly, it was very much in the interests of the entrepreneurs running the new industrial organisations that workers were mindful of customer needs (i.e. for a high-quality product) when the workers carried out their work. A crucial point, though, was that workers in the new great factories *no longer had any inherent emotional attachment to customers, because they had no contact with them.*

A handloom operator working in his cottage would be fully aware who his or her customers were; but once that worker was set to work inside a factory such as Arkwright's, the personal contact with customers was lost: in broad terms, the worker's only reason for wanting to do the best for the organisation's customers was fear of losing his or her job.

This trend towards the creation of large organisations, where most of the employees had little or no contact with customers continued until the 1970s, when a new revolution in technology occurred, causing radically novel changes in the way organisations interacted with their customers. I look at these changes later in this chapter.

The eighteenth century also saw the beginning of what we can identify as another major change in the relationship between organisations and their customers.

The cult of the customer

In the past, customers had always been vitally important, but the increasing wealth in Britain resulting from the Industrial Revolution, gradually created a new middle class that aspired to live, as far as it could afford it, in the style of the upper class. This trend was evident by the end of the eighteenth century but only truly blossomed in the nineteenth.

Businesses that catered for this new middle class found that there were enormous fortunes waiting to be made if the businesses could cater successfully to their needs, ideally on a large scale.

Many businesses that are still household names in Britain today started at around this time. The leading supermarket chain Sainsbury's, for example, traces its origins back to the founding, in 1869, by grocer John Sainsbury, of a grocer's shop in London.

John Sainsbury's success in those early days substantially derived from his innovative use of the newest form of transport — the railways — to bring in high-quality milk from the West country for his customers in London.

At the time, the lack of legislation regarding food quality meant that quality varied dramatically from one supplier to the other. There were cows in London: indeed, cows grazed in Hyde Park at around this time, and it was quite common for even the smartest London houses to be located close by a cow-shed, or to have one in their grounds. But milk produced from London's cows, fed as they were on fodder grown in London, or on fodder brought in from the countryside and unlikely to be very fresh or abundant, did not compare with milk brought in from the West country.

John Sainsbury's 'railway milk' became famous throughout London, his fame starting the growth of his business. The firm continued to grow, and by 1922 Sainsbury's was the largest food retailer in Britain. Later in the twentieth century the company pioneered self-service food supermarkets in the UK. Today, it is one of Britain's largest food retailers.

During the nineteenth century, the enormous revenues that could accrue to businesses which successfully met the needs of the new middle class, and the demanding nature of this middle class, led to what was indeed a cult of the customer. The customer became king (or queen), not only from the perspective of large businesses that supplied products and services to these customers but also from the point of view of small suppliers, who worked extremely hard to establish a clientele and, once they had won it, guarded it jealously.

Urban life in the nineteenth century, and especially in the major cities such as London, Bristol, Manchester, Glasgow and Edinburgh, saw the cult of the customer reach new and unprecedented heights. A massive infrastructure of suppliers served those who could afford it with everything they needed to run their houses, including all the foods that were consumed during an epoch when large, heavy and by our standards pretentious meals were the norm.

And that was only the food; a myriad of other domestic products were supplied to households, not the least extraordinary of which was lake ice, which – in this period before mechanical refrigeration had been invented – was cut from lakes by enterprising suppliers during the winter, kept frozen throughout the year in special stores rigorously insulated with materials such as hay, and sold to households as they needed it. So adept was the art of keeping ice that ships sending goods to Britons working in far-flung parts of the empire could store goods such as butter in lake-ice that remained frozen for the entire voyage.

Today, justly proud as we are of our highly complex societies with their rapid, often international, supply chains, it is easy to forget that the nineteenth century had its own remarkably complex sources of supply, and that enormous effort and industry were devoted to maintaining and broadening them. If any of us were catapulted back in time to, say, the middle of the nineteenth century, we would, I think, find the business world's infrastructure far more complex than we might imagine it would be. The people of the nineteenth century even had, in the telegraph system, a communications facility that had something in common with the internet, as the writer Tom Standage has pointed out in his book *The Victorian Internet* (1997).

Part of the proof of the existence of a cult of the customer in the nineteenth century was that it was a time when people were defined by their professions. Large-scale nineteenth-century maps of London, for example, give the names of the occupiers of houses along with their jobs. The obsession on what one did for a living – and a corresponding focus on the importance of customers – was understandable: it was a period when the lack of adequate welfare provision meant that lack of an occupation could easily mean starvation.

In *Oliver!* (1966), the movie version of Lionel Bart's highly popular twentieth-century musical of the same name, the scene featuring the song 'Who will buy?' beautifully, movingly and tunefully depicts a variety of traders parading the streets of London offering wares that include roses, milk, strawberries and a knife-grinding service.

Such traders did of course parade the streets, as well as call on individual houses. The scene is, in broad terms, an accurate depiction of what British towns and cities of the nineteenth century were like commercially: a huge number of suppliers offering their wares to customers who dwelled in the more prosperous parts of the towns and cities.

Householders today who shop at supermarkets, or on-line, for milk, butter, bread, meat, vegetables, potatoes and indeed almost anything that a household might want, would be surprised to find that in the nineteenth century all these staples, and many other goods too, were supplied to households by a door-to-door service devoted to pleasing that most precious of assets: the customer.

Even as late as the 1970s, doorstep delivery of some foods and services to households still occurred in a fashion that was like a whispered echo of how it had happened during the nineteenth century. However, during the 1970s, the introduction of supermarkets tended, generally, to put paid to that delivery channel... at least until the advent of today's home delivery of items ordered online from a supermarket's website.

In nineteenth-century literature, there are surprisingly few references to the cult of the customer and to the complexity of supply chains for doorstep delivery of everything a household might need. The entire works of Charles Dickens, for example, only make passing reference to suppliers of goods in London. Dickens, who has a great reputation as a chronicler of life in London, was actually more interested in its oddities and curiosities than in paying much attention to everyday commercial life. With only a few exceptions, everyday commercial life gets scant treatment in his books. Even his novel *Dombey and Son* (1848), which is about the head of a London-based international trading company, focuses almost entirely on personal relationships. There are barely half a dozen pages about business in the novel, and those pages only serve to show how little Dickens knows about the everyday realities of the *non-literary* commercial world. (He was an expert in the literary commercial world). He is not very interested in any area of business apart from the book and periodical business, rather as few novelists today would be likely to feature in their works many scenes involving visits to the supermarket.

However, what is also true is that Dickens, being wealthy from his writing from his mid-twenties, was a significant customer himself, and – as the twentieth century writer George Orwell pointed out – Dickens tends to see business life from a customer's perspective. When Dickens is thinking about life in this way, his writing about business suddenly comes alive.

There is no better illustration of this than in his wondrously vivid and jaunty account, in his masterpiece *A Christmas Carol* (1843), of the shops on Christmas morning that Scrooge is shown on Christmas morning by the Ghost of Christmas Present. The energy and passion which Dickens brings to this account of Victorian consumerism is a sort of orgy of the senses, as well as being a superb demonstration of the existence of a cult of the customer in the nineteenth century. Enjoy!

The poulterers' shops were still half open, and the fruiterers' were radiant in their glory. There were great round, pot-bellied baskets of chestnuts, shaped like the waist-coats of jolly old gentlemen, and tumbling out into the street in their apoplectic opulence. There were ruddy, brown-faced, broad-girthed Spanish Onions, shining in the fatness of their growth like Spanish friars;

and winking from their shelves in wanton slyness at the girls as they went by, and glancing demurely at the hung-up mistletoe. There were pears and apples, clustered high in blooming pyramids; there were bunches of grapes, made in the shopkeeper's benevolence to dangle from conspicuous hooks, that people's mouths might water gratis as they passed; there were piles of filberts, mossy and brown, recalling, in their fragrance, ancient walks through the woods; and pleasant shufflings ankle deep through withered leaves; there were Norfolk Biffins, squab and swarthy, setting off the yellow of the oranges and lemons, and, in the great compactness of their juicy persons, urgently entreating and beseeching to be carried home in paper bags and eaten after dinner. ...

The Grocers! Oh, the Grocers! Nearly closed, with perhaps two shutters down, or one; but through those gaps such glimpses! It was not alone that the scales descending on the counter made a merry sound, or that the twine and roller parted company so briskly, or that the canisters were rattled up and down like juggling tricks, or even that the blended scents of tea and coffee were so grateful to the nose, or even that the raisins were so plentiful and rare, the almonds so extremely white, the sticks of cinnamon so long and straight, the other spices so delicious, the candied fruits so caked and spotted with molten sugar so as to make the coldest lookers-on feeling faint and subsequently bilious. Nor was it that the figs were moist and pulpy, or that the French plums blushed in modest tartness from their highly-decorated boxes, or that everything was good to eat and in its Christmas dress; but the customers were all so hurried and eager in the hopeful promise of the day, that they tumbled up against each other at the door, clashing their wicker baskets wildly, and left their purchases upon the counter, and came running back to fetch them, and committed hundreds of the like mistakes in the best humour possible; while the Grocer and his people were so frank and fresh that the polished hearts with which they fastened their aprons behind might have been their own, worn, outside for general inspection...

I don't know exactly what the 'polished hearts' were: doubtless some long-forgotten fashion for apron fasteners, but the idea of grocery staff wearing polished hearts is as good a symbol as any of the nineteenth century passion for looking after customers' every whim.

Dickens's account of the shops on Christmas morning is an utter glorification of the nineteenth-century cult of the customer.

You can still get a sense of that cult today by visiting shops such as Harrods, Fortnum and Masons or John Lewis in the run-up to Christmas. In particular, the Harrods' food-halls especially very consciously — and rather successfully, too — preserve the Victorian atmosphere of plenty and of nothing being too much trouble for customers.

Dickens's account of the Christmas morning shops is actually quite rare in Victorian literature, and indeed in his own work. On the whole Victorian writers do indeed pay little attention to everyday commerce, seeing it as too familiar to bother much with.

But when everyday habits disappear and become part of history, they start to seem more interesting. By the start of the twentieth-century, when new ideas about social equality had begun to take root, people paid more attention to the cult of the customer and to the efforts suppliers took to meet practically every possible need of their customers.

The writer and former domestic servant Margaret Powell, for example, recalls in her hugely successful (and highly entertaining) 1968 memoir *Below Stairs* her life in domestic service in the 1920s in the seaside town of Hove in southern England. Her recollections recorded a way of life, with a cult of the customer — for whom no luxury was too luxurious, and no self-indulgence too excessive — that had, clearly, not changed greatly since the nineteenth century.

Mrs Clydesdale was the mistress of the house where Margaret Powell was working at the time, and Mrs McIlroy was the cook. Even the idea of a private household employing someone full-time as a cook will most likely seem profoundly alien to you today: that is, unless you've recently won a Match Six lottery jackpot without having to wait 51,000 years.

The amount of food that came into that house seemed absolutely fabulous to me, the amount of food that was eaten and wasted too. They often had a whole saddle of mutton. You don't see saddles very much now but they were gorgeous things. And sirloins. Sometimes with the sirloin they would only eat the undercut and the whole top was left over, so we used to have that for our dinner. Even so, we couldn't eat everything and a lot got thrown away. When I used to think of my family at home where we seldom had enough to eat, it used to break my heart.

The milkman called three times a day – at half past four to five in the morning he would leave some milk, then he would come round again at ten o'clock with more milk and any other orders that you wanted. Naturally, he carried cream and eggs with him, but if you wanted butter and cakes which he sold, or anything like that, he came yet again at about two o'clock in the afternoon.

I've never seen such milk and cream and eggs. Pints of cream nearly every day was nothing in that household, even when they weren't entertaining...

Most of the shopping was ordered from a grand shop in Hove, like Fortnum and Mason's, only you had to be a member to use it. I suppose in a way it was like a rich man's co-op. I don't know if you got a dividend.

They had departments for everything: greengrocery, butchery, cakes, and ordinary groceries.

Mrs Clydesdale would come down about ten o'clock and give cook her menus for the day, and if Mrs McIlroy wanted anything she hadn't already in, she would just ring up and ask them to send it round. That's all you had to do with tradesmen in those days. Just ring them up. In fact, the butcher and the greengrocer would come round for orders when they thought cook knew what she wanted for the day, and in less than half an hour they would be back with it.

Apart from the detail about the telephone calls – the telephone was only invented in 1876 and didn't begin to be fairly widespread even in affluent homes until the early years of the twentieth century – this recollection would have been applicable to any prosperous British household during the nineteenth century. Especially, one might add, in the second half of the century, when prosperity brought in by the Industrial Revolution and the success of the British Empire meant that rich people were very rich indeed.

Wealthy Victorians were pampered and enjoyed the cult of the customer to the full. Whether such pampering was good for their health was another matter. The abundance of milk, cream and eggs in Margaret Powell's recollection, coupled with the fact that meals were heavy on meat and fatty sauces and often concluded with toasted cheese, explains why many well-off Victorians – including Charles Dickens himself – never got to see their 60th birthday.

Margaret Powell mentions a 'grand shop' that was a department store for the wealthy. The shop to which she compares it, Fortnum and Mason's, was first established at 181 Piccadilly, London, in 1707. Like its great counterpart Harrods, in London's Knightsbridge, Fortnum and Mason's has always been a sort of temple for the customer.

Both these shops are still at their locations in Piccadilly and Knightsbridge, living reminders of the nineteenth-century cult of the customer. The great mills of the nineteenth century have passed into history, or have been converted into museums, trendy coffee-shops, or luxurious duplex apartments for the well-heeled. But many of the great retailer shops of the nineteenth century still exist today (and some, like Sainsbury's, have grown enormously).

The basic nature of the retail industry is pretty much the same today as it was in the past, mainly because the core business model is so straightforward and essentially simple. Retail was, and remains, a significant way to gain insight into the nature of the historical development of attitudes towards customer-centricity. So often we find that historical trends in retail get revisited and repeated: many modern retail chains consciously imitate 'old-fashioned' types of retailers: for example, some new chains of sweet-shops do this, and aim to sell old-fashioned types of sweets in shops that are competent reproductions of nineteenth-century sweet shops.

Even home deliveries, which never died out completely, have, as we've seen, been resurrected by the introduction of online shopping.

In the nineteenth century itself, the cult of the customer naturally led to a sort of corresponding cult in professional pride and expertise. Victorian standards of workmanship of decorative items, furniture and indeed of almost anything for which customers were prepared to pay, have arguably never been surpassed.

One legacy of this today is a wondrous inheritance of beautiful antiques that continue to surprise and delight and have inspired popular television programmes such as, in Britain, *Antiques Roadshow* and the TV drama *Lovejoy* (known as *The Lovejoy Mysteries* in the US).

Another legacy is an array of products that have come down to us as a direct result of nineteenth-century inventiveness, which – ardent to offer new, useful, attractions to customers – are based on inventions that took place not, as one might perhaps expect, in the twentieth century, but in the nineteenth.

The telephone, the typewriter, the camera, the transatlantic cable, the machine-gun and the rocket are all nineteenth-century inventions. The first transatlantic cable, laid in 1866, was used to send electric messages via the telegraph system, which indeed it is not fanciful to describe as a forerunner of the internet. Even the vacuum tube, which was the basis in the 1940s for the world's first digital computers, was actually invented back in 1881, in Thomas Edison's invention laboratory at Menlo Park, New Jersey. The invention of the vacuum tube, and indeed the simultaneous discovery of the electron, was a completely accidental result of Edison's efforts to trying to develop an efficient electric light bulb, efforts that were themselves the direct result of the cult of the customer.

People like Thomas Edison, masters of their profession, were legendary figures in the nineteenth century for their success as giving customers what they wanted. In the nineteenth century, a cult of professional expertise and excellence went hand-in-hand with the cult of the customer.

For example, in Dickens's novel *Our Mutual Friend* (1865), the character Mr Venus ministers, with all his professional zeal and technical skill, to the strange Victorian taste for stuffed animals, skeletons (including human ones), all manner of creatures (including human foetuses) preserved in bottles, and similar curiosities that to the modern taste seem unpleasant at best and ghoulish at worst.

Venus consoles himself in a current state of romantic disappointment by telling a visitor, Silas Wegg, about his professional skills.

> *'You seem very low, Mr Venus. Is business bad?'*
> *'Never was so good.'*
> *'Is your hand out at all?'*
> *'Never was so well in, Mr Wegg. I'm not only first in the trade, but I'm **the** trade. You may go and buy a skeleton at the West End if you like, and pay the West End price, but it'll be my putting together. I've as much to do as I possibly can, with the assistance of my young man, and I take a pride and pleasure in it... I've gone on improving myself in my knowledge of Anatomy, till here by sight and by name I'm perfect. Mr Wegg, if you was brought here loose in a bag to be articulated, I'd name your smallest bones blindfold equally with your largest, as fast as I could pick 'em out, and I'd sort 'em all, and sort your wertebrae, in a manner that would equally surprise and charm you.'*

Mr Venus's particular profession has all but ceased to exist today... although it is true that some people who work for large organisations, when they are required to be customer-centric, have all the vital enthusiasm of stuffed creatures.

Mr Venus, however, was genuinely customer-centric. Still, a man of Mr Venus's application would be welcome to customers anywhere, even if he would nowadays most likely need to find some other craft to which to apply himself.

Charles Dickens himself was a master of customer-centricity. If he were writing his novels today they would need to be shorter and punchier for customers familiar with fast-moving narratives on TV and in the cinema. Dickens's long novels, of which *Our Mutual Friend* was one, were about 375,000 words long, or about six times the length of *The Customer-Centric You*. (By the time you've got a – hopefully – useful perspective on customer-centricity, *Our Mutual Friend* has only just started to get going.) Dickens's novels were all first issued as serialisations either sold on their own, or incorporated in magazines that Dickens himself edited. This approach, and the brilliant but – plotwise – usually rather rambling novels that Dickens produced, suited customers during an age when evenings were long and dark, and devoid of much in the way of entertainment except for playing cards (*Monopoly*, *Scrabble* and *Trivial Pursuit* had not been invented yet) or listening to the piano or harmonium.

Families enjoyed sitting round a table in candlelight or in the light of oil-lamps (electric light in homes was a twentieth-century development) while the more literate members would read aloud from the latest episode of a serialised novel. Money was tight, and buying a monthly or weekly episode of a novel was a lot cheaper than buying an entire book, which in any case would not be available until the author had finished writing it and issuing the episodes, a process that could easily take two years.

It was a different society, a different world. Mr Venus was as customer-centric as his creator was, but if they were transplanted into today's society they could only have maintained their customer-centricity by changing the nature of their products very radically.

Another Victorian who was extremely customer-centric was the Victorian entrepreneur who presided over his mill, or – if he was especially successful – his mills. Richard Arkwright, in the eighteenth century, had shown how to set up, run and rule factories that could make the most of the new types of technology that had been invented for the textiles industry, and which were perfectly suited to being powered by steam or water. By the nineteenth century the profits that could be won by canny entrepreneurs had made factory-masters into legendary heroes of the business world. The Victorians never lost their enthusiasm for reading the often fairly fanciful accounts of their rags-to-riches stories in books that treated these heroes as if they were latter-day saints.

In reality, they were notoriously gruff, narrow-minded fellows, who like many successful people had done well through good luck as much as good judgement, but all the same it *is* true that they were often extremely customer-centric.

And now, without further ado — for he's been banging on my door ever since I started writing, and he is not at all the kind of gentleman to be kept waiting — let's meet Mr Tobias Hardcastle.

Tobias, when he's not knocking down office doors, lives in a large mansion of grey stone in a prosperous neighbourhood on the outskirts of Manchester.

The firm of which he's undisputed master, Hardcastle Knitwear Limited, and which employs more than five hundred people, is located in the northern English town of Salford, just over the River Irwell from Manchester.

It is a raw, autumnal Sunday afternoon in early October, 1865. Queen Victoria is on the throne and the pound is worth a pound. Abroad, a large number of foreigners, dwelling in what Tobias Hardcastle regards as nations that are little more than a Mistake, are being taught right and wrong by officers of the British Empire, who have the backing of the British army and the navy. Hardcastle regards both of these as impossible to defeat. Indeed, in his mind, history is simply a series of battles won by England.

An ample seven-course luncheon has been served by a number of servants and footmen to the Hardcastle family – who comprise Tobias, his simpering and self-effacing wife Elizabeth, his son Tom, and daughter Jenny.

Jenny has just made the mistake of tentatively enquiring whether her father will allow her young man, William, to meet him, as they wish to become engaged.

'And how does your *William* intend to support you, Jen?' Tobias demands, with his usual brusqueness.

'Papa, he loves writing poetry and wishes to be a poet.'

Tobias almost falls off his chair. Finally, he stands up, drawing his coat-tails up behind him as he always does when he wants to make a big point.

'*Poetry?*' he exclaims. 'Poetry? I'll tell you what poetry is. When my five hundred workers are all hard at work at their machines making money for me: that's what I call poetry!'

'So... you won't consider the possibility of my become engaged to William, papa?' Jenny asks, timidly.

'You get engaged to a poet? I'd sooner grasp hold of Hardcastle Knitwear Limited – lock, stock and barrel – and toss it all into the river!'

Jenny bursts into tears and flees to her room, where she consoles herself by re-reading the love scenes in *Our Mutual Friend*.

Tobias goes to stand in front of the blazing fire, his hands lifting his coat-tails so that the fire can warm his far from inextensive posterior. He delivers a lecture to Tom (who as the eldest son of a Victorian factory master, is, according to tradition, a wastrel) on the perils of idleness, in which the aphorism 'the devil finds work for idle hands' has featured substantially. Tom, a deeply sullen look on his face, is sprawled over the room's most comfortable sofa, avoiding his father's gaze.

Altogether this has not been an agreeable afternoon for Tobias Hardcastle. He is very much looking forward to the morning, when he will be at work again, and work is his favourite activity.

He never openly shows his pleasure at work, though, preferring to adopt a permanent frown to 'keep my hands on their toes', as he puts it, in a rather complex metaphor. He always refers – as it's usual to do in 1865 – to his workers as 'hands'. But somewhere deep inside his stony heart he loves touring his domain, watching his workers hard at labour, and listening to the incessant clicking of his hundreds of knitwear machines making money for him.

Also, the strange thing about Tobias Hardcastle – and the thing that interests us most about him as far as *The Customer-Centric You* is concerned, is that, despite his general intolerant manner, his short temper with subordinates, his readiness to sack a 'hand' for almost any infringement whatsoever of the factory's draconian rules, his inability to make his children see him as anything more than a wealthy tyrant, *he is indeed extremely customer-centric.*

Why? Well, because he knows all his customers – who include buyers employed by large drapery concerns, export merchants, and anyone else willing to pay for his knitwear – by name. He sometimes goes hunting with them.

He entertains them regularly at his club in Manchester over lunch or dinner. He listens hard to what they say about their changing needs, he discusses their own customers with them. He has won their admiration and respect as a man who knows the value of money and who drives a hard bargain, but who at least talks to them in their own language of power and business and who makes no effort to sell them what they don't want.

As for Hardcastle himself, his only real god is money and he knows that sparing no effort to keep his customers happy is the way for him to get it, so he *does* spare no effort to keep his customers.

Yet, at heart, Tobias Hardcastle is a dinosaur and so, despite his great success now and terrifying reputation, he is doomed to extinction.

Why is he a dinosaur? Well, because he is, in truth, only customer-centric with his business customers.

His hands work hard for him out of fear of the sack, not out of affection for him or because they feel part of an exciting enterprise that brings meaning to their own lives as well as to his.

He's a dinosaur because his young managers all speak ill of him behind his back; they are afraid of his wrath, too, and also scared of the sack. He's also a dinosaur because his family basically can't stand him. We have, after all, seen how implementing customer-centricity isn't only a matter of doing so in your professional life.

As for Tobias Hardcastle's son Tom – whom Tobias would dearly like to have had as his successor (Tobias has long yearned to call his enterprise Hardcastle Knitwear & Son Limited), he's been so browbeaten by 'the governor' during all his life, that what energy and spirit he once may have had within him have been all but squashed out of him.

Destiny has decreed that one night, in a couple of months' time, Tom is going to steal all the cash and securities he can find in his father's safe, head for London, enjoy a fine few weeks there among pleasurable company living off this haul, before fleeing overseas and spending the last few years of his life addicted to wine and to increasingly ragged pleasurable company in the poorer quarters of some French sea-port.

The point is, Tobias Hardcastle was customer-centric, but only in a limited way. He founded no dynasty, and generally speaking Victorian factory masters did not found dynasties. They were buried in expensive graves, and soon forgotten. As for the fortunes they had worked so hard to accumulate, these were generally – not always but very often – frittered away by descendants who were less hard-working, less competent... and above all less customer-centric.

But this was to a large extent the fault of the industrialists' themselves. Their brusque personalities and tyrannical natures inspired fear rather than an inspirational level of performance. By and large, the great industrialists did not create dynasties. Their commercial enterprises tended to die with them, or were run in a half-hearted way for some years by a son or sons who would rather have been soaking up the sun in Monaco and spending their inheritance there.

And this really is the point: *the nineteenth-century perspective on customer-centricity usually only worked in a constricted way.* It created a society where the cult of the customer ensured that those with money were treated like kings and queens by people – principally tradesmen and domestic servants – who did not in most cases especially like their customers but worked for them out of a fear of the sack and, very likely, starvation. Life felt pretty good for those at the top, and much of the time felt pretty lousy for everyone else.

Today, we can and must do better than this. But to understand where we are now, there is still an important part of the jigsaw missing. It's time to look at the sweeping changes in the relationship between organisations and their customers and which began to make themselves felt towards the end of the twentieth century.

Radical changes in perspectives on customers during the late twentieth century

The late twentieth century saw major new developments across all areas of commerce and industry that brought a new dimension to the relationship between organisations and their customers.

Just as with the Industrial Revolution in the middle of the eighteenth century, these new changes were spurred on by new technology.

The distance of time between the mid-eighteenth century and

the late twentieth naturally means that no-one can have personal experience of both sets of changes. Yet if that had been possible, it is likely that the two sets of changes would have seemed to have much in common. In particular, both sets of changes were massive in their implications, revolutionary in nature, highly significant throughout the economy, and potentially very lucrative to the organisations that pursued them.

The difference between the two types of change was this: in the middle of the eighteenth century, the application of technology to industry and, eventually, to commerce, *made* money by allowing much greater productivity... and having the spin-off consequences we have seen: that the relationship between workers and their customers became in many cases more remote.

The developments late in the twentieth century, however, allowed organisations to *save* money. Moreover, the implications for the relationship between organisations and their customers were not a spin-off, but the heart of the whole thing.

The developments in the late twentieth century were possible because of the invention of the microchip in the 1970s and, by the early 1980s, the widespread availability of computers that used these new processors and consequently offered enormous processing capacity and low cost.

The deployment of this new generation of ultra-powerful computers had major implications for all areas of industry and commerce, but especially for the relationships between organisations and their customers. Hand-in-hand with the implementation of much faster and cheaper computers went new advances in telecommunications technology that, in particular, allowed data communications networks to operate much more often in real-time (i.e. the communication was despatched the moment the message had been finalised) rather than off-line (i.e. the communication was only despatched when the system again went live), and there may have been a delay of even a few hours before the finalised message was sent.

The introduction of these new technologies had particular implications for relationships between organisations and their customers, especially for organisations – such as banks and other types of financial service organisations and also retailers – who had tens of thousands, or even several millions, of customers. However, the implications of the changes were highly significant across all areas of commerce and industry.

The new revolution in customer service occasioned by the introduction of new computer technology and telecommunication technology happened meant that, for the first time, organisations *were able to replace, on a large scale, physical locations where they made contact with customers with remote contact delivered by means of the new technologies.*

In the financial services sector, a major problem for providers had always been the cost of managing accounts, especially in the post-war period when increased affluence, and greater social equality throughout society, meant that far more people had bank accounts than had been the case before the War. In Britain by the 1980s, for example, about 84 percent of the adult population had bank accounts.

Greater social mobility had also created a situation where the old-style banking industry model, where you banked with a local bank and received your services from that branch, was becoming increasingly outdated.

Customers wanted ways of accessing their bank accounts when they were far from their branches, including when they were abroad. As well as this, the traditional relatively short business days of retail banks were being seen as increasingly inconvenient by blue-collar workers, far more of whom now had bank accounts than had ever been the case before. For example, even in the early 1980s, it was common for banks to open at 09.30 in the morning and close at 15.30, and Saturday opening had hardly started to happen yet.

The most obvious visual symbol of the revolution in customer service being fostered by the implementation of the new technologies and for which there was a significant demand by customers, was the automated teller machine (ATM): the familiar 'cash machine' or 'hole in the wall'. Traditionally, UK financial institutions were based in one particular locality or region and indeed frequently that region gave the institution its name. One example was the Halifax building society. By the 1980s the Halifax was a major financial institution, but many other UK institutions were still relatively small and operated in specific localities. As the 1980s progressed they were building up their own small networks of ATMs but if one of their customers was venturing to another part of Britain, there was no realistic way for the customer to access the institution's ATMs.

Initially the ATMs was simply seen as serving as an extension of a physical branch's opening times, but the exciting dynamic potential of ATMs to do far more than this was spotted by some ambitious young executives in banking who sensed that a real revolution in how banks delivered customer service was underway and wanted to be part of it.

One of the most ambitious and far-sighted of these young executives was Rob Farbrother, who in the early 1980s was working with the British building society the Abbey National (now Santander Bank) and energetically helping to automate the front desks of the building society's hundreds of UK branches. Farbrother, an extremely energetic, creative individual who also resolutely believes in getting details right, then went on to join the large US bank, Citibank, in London as its operations director.

As Farbrother says:

Citibank was keen to spearhead an attack on the more established UK banks, but wanted to do this not by creating expensive bricks and mortar service centres but rather by investigating how multi-functional ATMs could create a more cost-effective and customer-friendly service and then acting vigorously on this knowledge in a competitive sense.

He adds:

It was an exciting time to be in the banking business. It wasn't just that ATMs were being deployed for the first time, though they were. It was also that the potential for ATMs to feature in networks that would allow customers unprecedented new levels of utility had made me realise that this was an area I really wanted to explore.

Farbrother's exploration of this opportunity led him to leave Citibank and set up an organisation initially called Funds Transfer Sharing (FTS) which offered the cunning proposition of creating a nationwide ATM network to which a full range of financial institutions could belong and offer their customers the enormous benefit of access to a nationwide network.

Farbrother's business model for FTS involved the organisation catering for large institutions that could afford their own ATM network but which saw the need to extend these services by using other institutions' ATMs *and* also involved FTS catering for small institutions that wanted a more localised type of ATM network that was installed and managed by a service provider that had access to other, larger, ATM networks.

Eventually, an ATM network – known as LINK (which still exists today) – was created for the first category of financial service organisations, with Farbrother as the founder chief executive officer (CEO). Simultaneously, FTS was created for the second category of financial service organisations, with Farbrother as the founder CEO and shareholder.

Farbrother had considerable success with LINK, which attracted many larger institutions, while FTS proved simultaneously attractive to smaller institutions.

Farbrother continued to expand his business model globally, creating reciprocal arrangements with ATM networks in Spain, Portugal, Italy, France, Belgium and Japan. Farbrother's international initiative was in effect a response to customers' needs to use their own savings account cards abroad to obtain local currency in the countries they were visiting without the charges often imposed by such organisations as Visa and Mastercard; charges that Farbrother regarded as excessive.

ATMs and ATM networks in the financial services sector were one highly visible sign of a revolution in customer-centricity that is still continuing today. It is a revolution characterised by the combined use of powerful computer technology and telecommunications technologies, which have in many cases usurped the previous business model that involved customers being served by physical branches. Essentially routine transactions have more and more been taken out of physical branches and are delivered to customers remotely. In the 1980s the remote delivery method was real-time networks such as those that Funds Transfer Sharing ran, and also services delivered over the telephone.

By the mid-1990s, when the internet revolution alongside the email revolution began to create a virtual world as varied and complex as the real one, these new delivery channels came into being.

Call centres have also been important since around the mid-1990s, and the fact that call centre employees in developing countries such as India are paid far less than those in developed countries has led to a situation that we all nowadays tend to take for granted, but which if you think about it is rather strange: our needs as customers are frequently met from call centres in places such as India that are many thousands of miles from where we live. Whatever you think of the levels of customer service delivered by call centres – and, as we shall see, they frequently have some drawbacks attached to them due to the inherent way in which their customer service approach is structured – they are here to stay.

The consequences of this revolution in customer services, occasioned by the fundamental automation of many aspects of the customer relationship through the use of advanced computer technology and new types of telecommunications technology, continue to transform our world today. They mean that many things customers took for granted in the past are no longer possible.

For example, there was a time when you paid your utility bill by going into the local office of the utility company and making a payment over a counter or perhaps dropping the payment into some device that received it automatically. However, utilities companies in the UK and in many other countries no longer offer physical branches and everything must be done remotely by phone, email, via the internet, or indeed via Rob Farbrother's next entrepreneurial ventures – called PayPoint in the UK and PayShop in

Portugal, where Farbrother now lives. PayPoint and PayShop enable customers conveniently to pay their bill at the checkout of any of many thousands of retail outlets, ranging from local tobacconists to convenience stores and large supermarkets.

Just as the Industrial Revolution that began in the middle of the eighteenth century created a situation where, for the first time in history on a large-scale, workers and their customers were rendered significantly remote from one another both at a practical and conceptual level, the new revolution in customer service has created automated delivery channels that can save everyone's time, and can also save organisations the huge cost of setting up physical branches to deliver services, but where it is too easy for the interaction between customer and customer service operative to become remote and impersonal. It is too easy for customers of a call centre, for example, to be seen as just a name on the other end of a phone and not as human beings with their own needs and agenda.

As for the banking industry, the trend towards replacement of physical branches by a service delivered by means of remote automation was counteracted by the realisation that banks do need to have some physical location for selling financial services to customers. Also, the very nature of the banking industry means that there are many complex services where it is necessary for customers to meet the bank's staff physically. It is also difficult fully to automate the paying in of cash and cheques to an account although many banks do this with some success. Yet most banks that aim at national coverage like to have a branch in all towns of any significant size, and in cities. Branches clearly offer promotional advantage to banks, and this is seen as important because of the very fact that customers have a choice when it comes to which bank to use.

It might be asked why it is that utilities companies do not any more have physical branches in towns when they themselves are selling to customers who have a choice about which provider to use. The answer seems to be that the much simpler nature of the utility service does not create a situation where customers need to visit their utility company on a regular basis.

What does Rob Farbrother think about the current state of the revolution in remotely-delivered customer services that he helped to kick-start in the 1980s?

I believe we are now at the dawn of new innovations in technology that further extend opportunities for delivering customer service remotely. However, there are important improvements that need to be introduced if the full potential of this revolution is to be achieved. In particular, internet banking must be made much more secure so that there can be far more confidence in the security of conducting transactions over the internet. There also needs to be more attention given to providing a friendlier interface to the online presentation of groceries and other household goods on internet shopping sites. As well as this, internet shopping should be supported by a customer-orientated and dedicated call centre where practical help can be given. The personal touch of the customer choosing to deploy a web-cam image of the customer himself/herself and the call centre agent in a corner of the screen (via, for example, Skype or MSN Messenger) could enhance the communication. Delivery of goods and accuracy of the fulfilment of orders could also be improved, with logistics employed more effectively.

Conclusion

There have been more changes in human life, at a technological and social level, since the middle of the eighteenth century than there were since the beginning of human history. There have correspondingly been more changes in how organisations interact with their customers over the same period than there were since the beginning of human history.

Looking at customer-centricity from a historical perspective, we can identify the following three vital dynamics that are also highly relevant today:

1. Organisations passionately wanted to find ways of delivering customer service cost-effectively. Gradually it was realised

that self-service shops were far more cost-effective than shops where everything had to be fetched by a sales assistant. As for the custom of delivering things to the customer's doorstep, this was hardly cost-effective at all, though it has again become so now that on-line shopping is increasingly popular. Cost-effective service delivery is a particularly pressing requirements for organisations today and unquestionably plays some role in the disappointing calibre of many customer services that are delivered remotely.

2. The greater the extent to which organisations made use of remote means of communicating with customers, the greater the physical and emotional distance between organisations and their customers. The relationship between customers and organisations was itself placed in some fundamental jeopardy in the middle of the eighteenth century when the onset of industrialisation created factories whose workers would probably never meet a customer. However, compared with today, when not only will a customer service operative in a call centre most likely never meet customers but may well be located many thousands of miles from them, the customer-centricity challenge is clearly much more significant.

3. Today, the increasing proliferation of automated customer service delivery channels creates a potential for a 'multiplier' effect in the delivery of customer service.

What this means is that because these remote customer service delivery channels have the potential to deliver services to huge numbers of an organisation's customers, it follows that if the services that are delivered automatically have a high level of customer-centricity the organisation has the opportunity to win the hearts of an enormous number of customers promptly and decisively.

In the past, a truly customer-friendly market stall operator would probably only be able to win the hearts of a few dozen customers per day, even on his busiest days, but the power of remotely-delivered service channels is so great that an organisation that is truly customer-centric can delight thousands or even millions of customers, and can do this relatively quickly.

In other words, if you get customer-centricity right, you can create almost endless win situations for your organisations within a short timeframe and establish a major competitive impetus. The power of the technology used to deliver these remote service channels will be on your side. Conversely, if you get it wrong, you can alienate thousands or millions of customers just as easily.

This being so, we'd better get customer-centricity right! And this is why we now need to look at the crucial issue of adding value, which ultimately is going to be a major factor in determining customer-centricity.

3

WHY ADDING VALUE IS THE CORE OF CUSTOMER-CENTRICITY

Defining the concept of added value

All business activity on the planet is designed to meet *human needs*. Even business activity directed around providing food for the animals at a zoo, or indeed for your pet dog or cat, is really directed around the needs of the people who run the zoo, or around the needs of the owner of the pet. Business is a human phenomenon, not an animal phenomenon.

Within the world of business – which of course embraces products and services delivered by public services organisations as well as by profit-making organisations – added value is:

> *the benefit, perceived by the customer, that a customer gains from a particular product or service above and beyond the intrinsic 'face value' of that product.*

A useful example here is that of a mobile phone. On the face of it, a mobile phone is simply a piece of electronic technology. The mobile phone's added value, however, coupled with an airtime agreement, is a tool that the customer can use to manage his or her life.

In a similar kind of way, a television – on the face of it simply a piece of technology that enables broadcast images to be displayed, with synchronised sound, on a screen – offers its customers a window on the world.

You get the idea. Clearly, the more added value a product or service can offer, the more attractive the product or service will be.

Unfortunately, too many organisations, so far from delivering added value, barely even deliver the face value of what they purport to be offering. So often the question of whether or not they are delivering added value comes down less to a question of how effective their customer service delivery systems are (though this will be a factor) but down to the *personal attitude of staff*. Helpful staff who want to assist customers can deliver a far greater service quality than unhelpful staff, even if they are using the same customer service delivery systems. Basically, what is needed is what is often a *discretionary effort* (which may well be above and beyond what the staff member is expected to do to fulfil the terms of his or her employment). The provision of these levels of discretionary services is precisely what Mark Price is talking about in his Foreword to this book when he writes about a passion for customer-centricity being in the DNA of the staff at his organisation the John Lewis Partnership. The vast multitude of all the services we are offered nowadays in person, by phone or via the internet only work, only offer added value, if the customer service people who are delivering the service truly want to help customers.

I've suggested what added value actually is. The question now is, what exactly is it at a technical level? I'd say that it is: **something we can see, hear, feel, smell, touch or are aware of psychologically and emotionally and which we see as important to us and improving our lives.**

Even a book or a film fits in with this definition because while the book or film may give us enjoyable thoughts and memories (just as a piece of toast with butter and Marmite on it might do), the book or film itself was initially a tangible experience: something – if our senses were working normally – we saw or heard.

Added value and the difference between a customer's wants and a customer's needs

It is important at this early stage in discussing added value to distinguish between what a customer *wants* and what a customer *needs*.

On the face of it, they are both equally important when looking at customer-centricity: after all, it is not our job, as providers of customer-centricity, to tell a customer what they should or shouldn't buy. If your job is to sell people luxury watches, you are hardly likely to be doing yourself or your career prospects any good if you point out to a customer who wants to buy a watch from you and has a mobile phone that they don't actually need to buy a watch as their mobile phone will do a perfectly good job of telling them what time it is.

This said, distinguishing between wants and needs can indeed be useful as a way of furthering the level of customer-centricity we are providing, because by drawing a distinction between the two we can often end up delivering customer-centricity more *precisely* than would otherwise have been the case.

A *need* is something that genuinely improves a customer's life

A *want* is something the customer desires, or think he or she does.

A customer may say they want something when in fact what they need is something different. The difference between a perceived need and a perceived want arises from:

- a lack of information on the part of the customer
- the fact that customers often make decisions based on emotions rather than logic

As providers of customer-centricity, it is our job to know what the customer really needs. If we are selling luxury watches, we know that customers buy these because they want to feel they are high-status individuals. This same thinking applies to many luxury products.

But if you are seeking to please customers in situations where your resources for delivering customer-centricity are limited, such as if you are working for a local authority that provides health services, your knowledge of customer needs is very important.

For example, an elderly, infirm person may say to a local authority, 'I need someone to help me get out of bed in the morning and make my breakfast for me'.

A social worker who knows the person, however, may be aware

that this is a want rather than a need, and may suspect that if the local council does supply someone to help the person get out of bed in the morning and make the person's breakfast, this may just lead to a deterioration in the person's independence.

Instead, the social worker may know the person well enough to know that what they *really* need is some companionship during the day.

This identification of the customer's real needs will very likely greatly help the local council to provide *efficient* customer-centricity that makes the best use of what will inevitably be limited resources, especially when they are being provided by a public sector organisation.

The better you know your customers, the more adeptly you can distinguish between a customer's wants and a customer's needs, and the better you can deliver to them what they really regard as added value.

How you can decide whether a customer will regard something as constituting added value

When deciding whether or not a particular product or service constitutes added value, it is useful to apply three questions to the situation.

1. Is the customer prepared to pay for and/or invest in the time or activity?

This is a vital initial question to apply to a situation. It's important to remember that the customer may be paying for the activity without being conscious of it. For example, a 'free' helpline is of course not really free; its cost is embodied in the cost of the product or service being sold. The question is important for many reasons, not least because there is a difference between something being an integral part of the service and the customer perceiving it as adding value. An everyday example of this is the security that an operator in a call centre does with you before proceeding with the call. You will probably find the security check boring or even irritating but the call cannot go on without it. However, a customer cannot expect to have to see the security check as part of the added value.

2. Does the activity improve something from the customer's perspective?

If it does, we can be sure that the activity will be perceived by the customer as adding value.

3. Is the activity being completed accurately first time?

This may seem a rather obscure question but it is actually extremely important. An activity that a customer will perceive as adding value if it is completed accurately *the first time* will very likely cease to be perceived as adding value if it has to be repeated.

For example, a customer who calls a helpline and then feels obliged to make the call again because the customer does not feel that all his questions were answered first time is unlikely to regard the second call (or successive calls) as constituting added value.

These three questions can be applied and used in either of two ways.

Firstly, you could take the view that if the answer to any question is negative the activity cannot be customer-centric.

Secondly, you could use the questions more informally to assess the activity for its customer-centricity.

The need to set moral considerations aside when assessing added value

I've already made the point that as providers of customer-centricity, it is not part of our job to make moral judgements.

This point needs emphasising because we need to discuss the concept of added value without involving moral considerations.

There are many things that people like to buy which I don't like to buy personally and which you won't like to buy personally. There are also things that people like to buy which I positively abhor and which I am sure you would abhor. But, again, moral consideration isn't the issue. The discussion is about what value added means, not whether you or I think what is being offered is good for the customer.

This point about moral considerations is important because it provides a useful introduction to the inescapable notion that when we are discussing added value, it's the customer's *conceptualisation* that really matters.

Let's again bear in mind what Professor David Thomson had to say earlier about the difference between *perception* and *conceptualisation*. As we saw, he draws a clear distinction between:

- what a sensory signature *is* – which he calls *perception*
- what a sensory signature *means* – which he calls *conceptualisation*

The same thinking Professor Thomson applies to sensory signatures can also be applied to added value. We could say, for example, that what the added value is might be termed the *perception* of that added value, while what the added value means to the customer might be termed the *conceptualisation*.

And conceptualisation of a perception is indeed the key to the whole subject of added value. Just as the whole focus of this book is on accepting the importance of the agenda of others, it is the conceptualisation of others that matters here.

To return to the Red Bull example: I personally do not like the drink and would never buy it for myself, but I accept that three million people or so every day do like the drink and buy it because, I suppose, as well as liking the taste and the boost of energy they derive from the ingredients they enjoy how the drink makes them feel emotionally and socially.

Professor Thomson has this to say about the link between conceptualisation and added value. He relates this discussion to a specific example – Red Bull. Certainly, the points he makes here are easier to understand when applied to a specific example.

As I see it, it's the manner in which we conceptualise something that delivers added value. So, for example, if Red Bull is conceptualised as being (for example) 'cool' (in the cultural sense of being fashionable, trendy and exciting), 'adult' and 'edgy', and that's what people want, then these conceptualisations are 'adding value'. Red Bull could be categorised as an 'added value' brand if consumers generally felt this way about the brand, especially if other energy drinks brands are failing to deliver this. I also think that the notion of 'added value' is conceptualisation but this is acting at a higher level (i.e. as an overview).

Clearly, this is leading-edge and pioneering thinking that could form the basis of extensive further thought and study. Professor Thomson goes on to suggest:

Perhaps 'added value' works at two levels. Level 1 is where consumers make conceptual associations with the brand/product etc. and these associations effectively 'add value' but perhaps in an overt or non-conscious manner. Level 2 is where the consumer forms an overview about the object in question which they consciously interpret as 'added value' (i.e. the conceptualisation of added value.)

This idea of a two-level conceptualisation of added value relating to a specific brand – a kind of particular conceptualisation and a more general conceptualisation – makes good sense. It might explain, for example, why we are disappointed if a brand in which we have a high general opinion due fails to deliver somehow. While food and drink brands are usually carefully kept unaltered, brands in other areas – music and movies, for example – will be generating new incarnations: as when a musician we like releases a new CD or a movie star we like stars in a new movie.

If we find the new CD or the new movie disappointing we may in effect feel that we cannot conceptualise the particular new incarnation of the brand in the positive way we would like to have done, but we may still have enough faith in the musician or movie star to be prepared to listen to or see their *next* CD or movie.

In any event, the intimate link between conceptualisation and added value is clear, and I am grateful to Professor Thomson for supplying the crucial terminology of conceptualisation.

Moreover, we must respect a customer's conceptualisation even if we believe that customers are positively wrong in how they conceptualise something. Their conceptualisation is what matters and, again, we must respect that.

Fortunately, in most customer-centricity contexts, one doesn't encounter major moral dilemmas. One sees an organisation offering a legal product or service which, clearly, some customers perceive as adding value to their lives.

The very fact that we talk about adding 'value' itself emphasises that it is conceptualisation that really matters. The value of something is only what people think it is worth.

At the close of the nineteenth century, when Vincent Van Gogh was still a struggling painter driven half mad by loneliness and malnutrition, the value of his paintings was regarded as minimal even by those who bothered to take a look at them. Today, when the paintings have actually deteriorated physically in the sense that they are now more than a century old, the value attached to them is so great that for the price of a single Van Gogh painting you could buy a substantial country estate.

Of course, some things have a more objective kind of value. If you are ill because you are suffering from a disease caused by bacteria, you will probably feel that antibiotics have an objective value to you that have little to do with your conceptualisation of them.

Enhancing an objective benefit so that the particular brand of the benefit an organisation is offering is conceptualised in an exciting way is exactly what most advertising is all about.

Why we must accept that the conceptualisation of added value only relates to the 'tip' of what is perceived

We've already seen that it isn't useful to bring a moral sensibility into the equation when we look at added value. It's also important to accept that perception of added value is very often only accorded to the most visible element of what may be an extremely complex process.

The experience of travelling by plane also provides a useful illustrative example here. When a customer books a flight with an airline (whether or not through a third party) the customer will in almost all cases only conceptualise the valued added as consisting of things directly relating to the experience of booking the flight and being conveyed to their destination.

The tone of the airline's customer service operative on the phone, the check-in at the airport, the friendliness of the cabin staff, the on-board food, the comfort of the seat, and so on, will be the factors that the customer sees as offering a benefit, along with the flight itself.

All the other things that were necessary in order to make the flight take place will – except in exceptional circumstances where the customer thinks about these things – are unlikely to be conceptualised as adding value. The design and manufacture of the plane and its engines and fittings; the nature of the fuel it uses and the need to retrieve the fuel from an oil well and refine it; the whole complex business of running the airport; the highly professional skill of air traffic control: these and many other factors will not be part of the customer's mindset when it comes to assessing value.

But of course all these other things have to be paid for, and ultimately the payment will be made by the customer even though the customer will not normally be conscious of this.

Indeed, the limited nature of the customer's perception of what does constitute added value only serves to show just how narrow that band of perception, which only focuses on what might be described as the 'tip' of the customer experience, really is. All the same, we have to accept this fact and accommodate it in our thinking about added value.

The changing nature of conceptualisation relating to added value

We need to bear in mind that what customers conceptualise as constituting added value will change over time, and that sometimes the time-frame for change will be very brief.

Any activity relating to fashion provides obvious examples of this. A pop star who is all the rage this week could easily be regarded as ancient history in a few months or even in a few weeks. As for clothes fashion, the very fact that something is fashionable now generally militates against it being fashionable for very long.

But it's not only changes in fashion that lead to changes in the conceptualisation of added value. In fact, changing conceptualisation of added value is a major challenge for any organisation that wishes to be customer-centric and I look at these challenges in the next chapter. For the moment, it is enough to mention that conceptualisation of what is regarded as value added will change.

When a new technology becomes available, it is routine that in the early days the conceptualisation of value added will focus to a large extent on the technology itself, but as people get used to it, the value-added conceptualisation will focus on other factors.

Aviation provides us with a compelling example of this. When air travel was first available, passengers had little choice but to be very much aware of the experience of the flight. If the plane had an open top they would even have had to wear goggles. Nowadays, when the likelihood of the plane getting you to your destination is taken for granted, people are more likely to be concerned about what in-flight movies are being screened; indeed, many modern jet airliners are essentially a sort of flying cinema.

In much the same way, when television first became available on a widespread basis in the early 1950s (the event that induced many people to rent or buy a television for the first time was the Coronation of Queen Elizabeth II in 1952), people were extremely conscious of the technology, partly because neither televisions nor the quality of the broadcast signal were very reliable.

Television is, in fact, an almost miraculous invention in which a tiny point of light is flashed electronically across numerous lines on a screen so fast that our eyes are deceived into thinking we are seeing a complete moving image. No inventor of TV can see as fast as his or her creation can operate. Colour television is even more miraculous. But of course hardly anyone thinks of that nowadays: television technology is extremely reliable and all people regard as constituting added value are the programmes.

Added value and customer-centricity

The overall relationship between added value and customer-centricity is this: **if your customers don't attach a conceptualised added value to the products or services you are offering them then you can't possibly be customer-centric.**

Yes, added value really is the core of everything in customer-centricity.

On one level this point is straightforward enough, which is why you won't try to sell a steak pie to a vegetarian, or a comb to a bald man.

But these are admittedly fairly extreme examples. In practice, understanding just how you or your organisation is adding value to a customer's life is as important as understanding exactly what you are offering the customer. Indeed, the two dynamics are intimately related.

Understanding where you are adding value requires not only an empathy with the customer's agenda but also a genuine interest in, and comprehension of, all the social, economic, cultural and historical factors that affect the lives of your customers.

This is, of course, only another way of saying that the more you understand your customers, the more likely it is that you can be customer-centric.

On the face of it, this is a straightforward and simple principle to learn. Know your customers and you'll be customer-centric. But if it is such a simple principle, why is a genuine desire to be customer-centric so rare both among organisations and among individual people?

This is a vitally important question, and addressing it deserves a chapter to itself.

4

THE DYNAMICS *OPPOSING* CUSTOMER-CENTRICITY

Central to my thinking on customer-centricity is my belief that for the vast majority of people, being customer-centric is unnatural. I think it is unnatural because evolution, who is – I'm afraid – single-minded in pursuing *her* agenda and cruel as well as talented, has programmed us to be selfish.

There are also some inherent practical reasons that inhibit customer-centricity.

Overall, I believe that the dynamics which inhibit customer-centricity are these:

- the sheer psychological factor that people are not naturally customer-centric in their thinking
- the problem that as organisations grow they tend to focus excessively on their own agenda
- the problem that the nature of customer demand changes, and sometimes changes quickly
- the problem of cost

Let's look at these factors in turn.

The sheer psychological factor that people are not naturally customer-centric in their thinking

I think there's little choice but to accept that a major factor which inhibits customer-centricity relates to the individual psychology of most people, who simply don't care enough about the customers in their lives – especially the customers they have in their professional lives.

This may indeed be the fault of evolution rather than the people themselves, but just blaming it on evolution hardly helps. After all, evolution – and the bodies and minds it has presented us with – is only the starting-point. We have the luxury of taking responsibility for our own attitudes towards evolution.

For many people – probably indeed for the majority – their indifference to others is such that the very notion of customer-centricity is not something that would come naturally to them, let alone the idea of taking part in a structured exercise to make some particular organisation customer-centric.

In most cases, considerable effort is needed in most cases, to bring people round to developing a customer-centric mindset.

The next chapter looks in detail at the customer-centric mindset, which I believe is a mindset that can be acquired if one *wants* to do so. (Indeed, I think one can improve one's skill in very many respects if one *wants* to do so.)

But if someone has no real interest in the customers in their lives, and *doesn't want* to take any more interest in them, there isn't much that can be done without significant coercion. Yet in practice, as you are reading this book, it's a safe assumption that you yourself already have a real interest in customers and their agenda. However, as there will possibly be people in your team who don't, I point out here the two remedies to this problem of indifference to customers.

The first remedy is, clearly, that people can be *inspired* to get better at being customer-centric. People can be persuaded to see that being customer-centric will make their own lives better in all respects and happier.

The second remedy is that, in work situations at least, people can readily be made to understand that if they *don't* get into the customer-centricity mindset, they are likely to lose their jobs, or at least not make the progress with their careers that they would like to make.

If you're heading a team of people, whatever the size of that team (including a major organisation with hundreds or even thousands of staff) it is inevitable that there will be people in your team who, whatever their technical skills, will not be as naturally in tune with the agenda of customers as they should be.

Yes, they can to some extent be *compelled* to be more caring of customers' agenda, but it is far better that they are *inspired* to be caring of that agenda, and my aim in the next chapter is to provide material that can help towards that vitally important aim.

In the meantime, all there really is to say is a reiteration of the point that while a compelled interest in customers' agenda is certainly better than nothing, an interest in customers that springs from a person's own inclinations (or, following inspirational intervention, the person's new take on life and others) is much better.

Shakespeare's views of human life have only seemed truer during the four centuries or so since he wrote his plays. He has something to say about most aspects of life, and this is no exception. In his play *Twelfth Night*, Olivia observes:

Love sought is good, but given unsought is better.

Which is also true of the kind of general love of one's fellow human beings that is the well from which customer-centricity springs. Put into customer-centricity terms, we can say that being customer-centric because you know you will lose your job if you aren't *is* (of course) better than not being customer-centric at all. But being *naturally* customer-centric because that's what you're like as a person and because you don't need any coercion to be customer-centric, is much better.

The problem that as organisations grow they tend to focus excessively on their own agenda

Many of us have at some point in our careers helped to run a small business, or a semi-autonomous department of a larger business, which can amount to much the same thing. Don't you remember the buzz you had when you went to work? The excitement on Sunday evening of looking forward to getting in on Monday morning and making things happen?

How often do people running small businesses or a semi-autonomous department of a larger business, ignore the customer's agenda? Not often, because quite apart from the inevitable pressing financial incentive to meet customers' needs, the *physical and emotional proximity* of the customer makes it much easier to generate customer-centricity than when one is working within a large organisation.

In effect, anyone running a small business, or a semi-autonomous department of a larger business, is rather like the people who ran most businesses before the onset of the Industrial Revolution. At that time, as I've suggested, there usually wasn't a major challenge as far as customer-centricity was concerned, because suppliers knew their customers well, and the small scale of the business enterprises they were running meant it was easy for the business to focus on its customers than on its own agenda.

Mark McCormack, in *What They Don't Teach You at Business School*, has some pithy and well-made observations about what it's like running a small but growing business. These are drawn from his own recollection of the early days of the sports agency he created, IMG, when he and his team were representing, among others, great golfers like Arnold Palmer and Gary Player. He talks of the thrilling entrepreneurial feeling he had when he started out:

There is no other feeling like that in business, or at least any that I have ever experienced. It's not just the excitement, although that is certainly part of it. It is more a sense of the immediacy and importance that everything takes on, the feeling that what you do from day to day matters, and generates a desire to do even more.

It also brings with it a certain amount of anxiety. It's hard to feel complacent in a tiny new company, because in the back of your mind you're always wondering if you're still going to be around in six months. It puts an edge on everything you do. I wanted, if possible, to avoid a bureaucratic structure that would dull this edge.

*There is also an **ésprit** in small growing companies which is difficult to explain to anyone who has never experienced it. I suspect it is not unlike the feeling ones gets from being a member of a champion sports team, a satisfaction that comes from contributing to something larger than yourself. In the early days, when Arnold or Gary would win a tournament over the weekend, everyone would come in to work so pumped up on Monday mornings there would literally be races for the telephones. I knew, however, that if we were to grow we would soon have people working for us who wouldn't know a putter from a wedge, much less who won over the weekend.*

*I knew this special **ésprit** could not be totally preserved, but certainly part of it could, and I wanted a structure that would help us achieve that. The key, I felt, was to think small, to structure something that would make everyone feel like a very big cog in his or her respective wheel.*

Actually, I don't quite understand why Mark McCormack felt that the day would come when he'd have people working for him who didn't know about golf. I would indeed like to know what he felt that, but sadly he isn't around any more for us to ask him. Perhaps when he wrote his great book the job market was less tough, and you couldn't expect always to hire people who were really into what your organisation is doing. Nowadays, though, when competition for jobs is intense, you *can* certainly expect to hire people who are really into what you're doing, as indeed they should be.

Unfortunately, in many cases, perhaps even in most cases, the larger an organisation grows the worse it becomes at devoting itself to customers.

Research that Charteris has carried out suggests that in many large organisations, only about *30 percent* of activity is devoted to customers' interests. The other 70 percent? Well, it consists of stuff that isn't, stuff that's about the organisation's agenda – often simply internal stuff – rather than what's focused around the customer.

There you go: there's the gap between what people *know* and what they actually *do*.

After all, it's not as if these people who go to work and devote themselves purely to the organisational agenda think 'customers aren't important'. But all the same, some passion for the customer has slipped away, some customer focus that should be as taut as a bowstring has become slack and loose, some disease of indifference to customers has contaminated the organisation.

As an organisation grows in size, its customers become increasingly remote physically and emotionally from the people who work at the organisation. This has been a problem since the earliest days of industrialisation.

Also, when an organisation is becoming larger and more complex, it accumulates more and more of its own internal 'stuff' that it wants to focus on.

This is more of a problem today than it was in Richard Arkwright's day, when there was little legislation affecting large organisations, as governments adopted a *laissez-faire* (= 'leave alone') attitude towards business. Today, organisations must operate during a climate of intense regulation.

Also, the dictatorial nature of business leadership, under people like our friend the Victorian industrialist Tobias Hardcastle, tended to keep organisations more focused on meeting the needs of customers than today, when the much greater complexity of the commercial, economic, legal and technological frameworks require a correspondingly more collaborative and sophisticated approach to management.

In any case, no organisation can afford to use the excuse that its size means it needs to focus on its own internal stuff rather than on its customers. Any organisation that thinks like that is most likely simply too lazy to take the trouble to look hard at itself and strip away the dead wood from its processes so that the whole organisation becomes customer-centric.

In the movie *Wall Street* (1987), the businessman Gordon Gekko's 'Greed is good' speech has become famous, partly because of its appeal to people who do believe that greed is good and find Gekko's speech excellent support for their own philosophy of life, such as it is.

Yet it's also true that the popular perception of Gekko's speech takes it radically out of context. In the particular scene where it appears, Gekko's speech seems much less a sort of gratuitous hymn to greed and much more a justified attack on the complacent, inefficient, wasteful, self-centred paper company on behalf of whose shareholders he is speaking. He is arguing that the paper company has been giving an extremely raw deal to the shareholders and judging from the evidence he presents he is dead right. And, after all, for any publicly-listed company, its shareholders are an absolutely vital, though specialised, segment of its customers.

Gekko was making his speech at a shareholders' meeting of an ailing paper company whose shareholders were indeed unhappy with its performance, and Gekko was emphatically on the side of the shareholders. As far as he could see, a major cause of the paper company doing so badly was that it was so caught up with its own agenda and the self-indulgences of its senior executives:

You are all being royally screwed over by these... these bureaucrats with their luncheons, their hunting and fishing trips, their corporate jets and golden parachutes... Teldar Paper has 33 different vice presidents each earning over $200,000 a year. Now, I have spent the last two months analysing what all these guys do, and I still can't figure it out. One thing I do know is that our paper company lost $110 million last year and I'll bet that half of that was spent in all the paperwork going back and forth between all these vice presidents.

Gekko was brash and a crook, but he was at least right in one respect: if organisations want to do their best for their shareholders, they need to eliminate their internal efficiencies and their self-indulgences.

In our terminology, they need to infuse themselves with customer-centricity.

Instead of large organisations devoting about 30 percent of their efforts to their customers and the remaining 70 percent to their own agenda, the proportions need to be reversed.

Sir Isaac Newton devised three laws. In this book I'll modestly only propose two. I'll call the first, reasonably enough, Hewett's First Law. It's this:

No organisation can be customer-centric unless it is devoting at least 70 percent of its efforts and energies exclusively to the agenda of its customers.

This law, by the way, applies to all organisations, public sector ones as much as profit-making ones. Devoting that 70 percent of effort to customers is not _the only thing_ you need to do if you are to infuse your organisation with customer-centricity, but it's certainly a great way to start.

It's important to emphasise that the 30 percent of efforts that _is_ devoted to the organisation's own agenda is _not_ something the organisation should be ashamed of. This 30 percent will most likely be essential and without it the organisation probably could not offer the 70 percent of its effort to customers.

This said, I am not going to compromise on my belief that devoting any more than 30 percent of organisational energies to the organisation's own agenda is a disastrous mistake, and will mean that the organisation cannot be customer-centric.

The problem that the nature of customer demand changes over time, and sometimes changes quickly

As we saw in the previous chapter, customers' conceptualisation of what constitutes added value is the core of customer-centricity. You can only be giving customers what they want if you are satisfying their conceptualisation of what constitutes added value.

This is a crucial point. It is also vital to bear in mind that, as we also saw, customers' conceptualisation of what constitutes added value changes over time, and sometimes quickly. The nature of customer demand consequently also changes.

In practice, this tendency for customer demand to change is the another major factor opposing customer-centricity, for the very straightforward reason that what an customer regards as meeting its needs *now* will not be sufficient to meet the customers' needs when those needs change.

What customers regard as constituting added value changes for many different reasons. We can identify two types of changes: *macro changes* which relate to society as a whole, and *customer-oriented changes* which relate to individual customers.

Macro changes include changes in:

- economic factors
- central and local government
- social structure
- social behaviour
- technology
- the environment

Customer-oriented changes include changes in the following factors relating to customers' personal circumstances (listed in what I regard as the order of their importance to organisations seeking to meet customer demand):

- financial circumstances
- health
- age
- educational level
- career progress
- marital status
- parental status
- geographical location
- access to communications tool
- access to transport
- access to the organisation at a physical level

Taken together, macro changes and customer-oriented changes constitute significant and continual modifications to what the customer regards as constituting added value.

The only realistic way for an organisation that wants to be continually customer-centric to proceed is for it to *be, as far as possible, constantly aware of the nature of the changing demand,*

and to strive at all times to be able to answer the question 'where and how am I adding value for this customer?'

The problem of cost

The more customers an organisation has, the more complex their needs will be and the more difficult it becomes to meet those needs cost-effectively. We need to bear in mind that many organisations would in fact like to become more customer-centric, but are operating in fiercely competitive market environments where cost pressures can too easily dampen enthusiasm for customer-centricity and its practical implementation.

All the same, cost is too often used by organisations as an excuse for not performing well on the customer-centricity front. After all, the organisation is in business to serve its customers, and if it is in effect saying *'intense competition in our markets makes it too expensive for us to serve our customers properly'* then it should look at ways of streamlining its activities in order to reduce its costs so that it *can* serve its customers properly. Otherwise the very fact that there *is* intense competition in its sector is likely to drive it out of business.

In practice, I have repeatedly found in my own consulting work that when an organisation is streamlined and re-structured in order to become more customer-centric, it tends to enjoy not *only* a new and much improved relationship with its customers, but *also* reduced costs throughout its entire operational and administrative base.

I look in Chapter 7 at the exciting and wonderful double whammy of achieving better customer service delivered at reduced costs.

Conclusion

Being customer-centric requires the right attitude *and* the right action if we are to overcome the factors that tend to oppose customer-centricity.

These factors can be overcome, but they must never be underestimated.

What is certain is that we can only be customer-centric in the first place if we have the right attitude, the correct mindset.

Let's now look at it.

5

THE CUSTOMER-CENTRICITY MINDSET

Initial thoughts

In this chapter, while focusing on the need to develop the customer-centricity mindset now, in the present, I draw liberally on ideas from the past – including some literary ones – to investigate the whole question of what constitutes the customer-centricity mindset and how one can acquire it.

These cultural sources are of vital importance in this chapter. The point is that the need to care about the agenda of others is not (of course) only a commercial requirement, but also a social one. As the columnist Christina Patterson pointed out in the passage I quoted above, society cannot function well if we only care about the people in our family.

As for the cultural references I use in this chapter, the truth is that there is a very real sense in which acquiring the customer-centricity mindset is all about re-learning – rediscovering – lessons and inspirations about how we ought to be towards one another. These lessons and inspirations have been learned in the past, but are all too easily forgotten amidst the hubbub and pressures of modern life, which make it, in particular, far too easy to forget that we should care about strangers... and *why*.

Why we should care about strangers

I suggested in the previous chapter that our evolution has made us selfish.

I'd qualify that by adding that evolution has made us particularly selfish *in relation to people who are strangers to us*. In regard to people who are close to us we are often comparatively unselfish, though as I suggested at the start of this book, our apparent unselfishness in relation to people we love or to whom we are otherwise close in a personal sense is very likely partly practised for selfish reasons, because we want their love and admiration.

Very well, perhaps you will think I am being too cynical here, and you may be right, but what I do not think you will doubt is that most of us are pretty selfish when it comes to caring about the agenda of strangers. Caring about the agenda of strangers does not come naturally. Saints do it, Mother Theresa did it, but very likely you are not a saint, and you certainly aren't Mother Theresa.

Caring about the agenda of strangers indeed *doesn't* come naturally, but this is what we have to do if we want to infuse ourselves (and, if applicable, our organisations) with customer-centricity.

In fact, caring about strangers makes sense, if you think about it, for reasons other than that you want to be customer-centric.

Indeed, if you think about it, *not* caring about strangers is what makes little sense. After all, strangers have built the world for us...

Go to YouTube and find one of many videos of the immortal Louis Armstrong singing *What a Wonderful World*. He truly cares about strangers in that song; doesn't he make *you* want to care about strangers, too?

Let's indeed think about that wonderful world for a while.

Our world, and the universe around it, is composed of two elements and two elements only: the natural world we inherit, and the human world containing everything human beings have built in – the buildings, the transport networks, the houses, the machines, the tools, *everything* that other people have built for us, or we have built for ourselves.

And this is the point: without other people's efforts on behalf of us, the only things there would be in the human world would be what we made ourselves. Even the most industrious of people would have scarcely anything to call their own. We are utterly reliant on the efforts of others to have the things in the world that we need.

Here I am, writing using a word-processor that I didn't make that uses computer software I didn't design and which prints out the results of my day's efforts using a computer printer, toner and paper, none of which I played the slightest part in manufacturing.

My word-processor and printer use electricity I didn't generate that originates from coal I didn't mine or from nuclear fuel I didn't process to a state where it is useable in a reactor I didn't build. That electricity flows to my house though cables I didn't lay. I did not make any of my clothes, nor anything at all in my writing room.

I've just done a quick count and found that my writing room contains about 700 things – including computer devices, telecommunications devices, different types of document, books (including my copy of *Teach Yourself to Write an Inspirational Business Book* – no, only joking), magazines, cups, tea-cups, furniture, a carpet, a rug, a radiator and so on, and so on – none of which I made myself, though I have produced some of the documents.

Without all these things, my writing-room would not be what it is, and without quite a few of these things I couldn't write this book at all.

Even our justifiable conceptualisation of ourselves (when we bother to think about this) as the extremely fortunate inheritors of two centuries or so of remarkable, even close to miraculous, technological progress is completely dependent on the prodigiously varied and complex chain of activity that keeps our technological world supplied with all the software, systems and hardware that it needs to function.

We have a romantic view of inventors that they are brave, lone individuals struggling to get some new idea off the ground – literally, in the case of the Wright Brothers.

Of course, there *are* inventors like that, who make the crucial initial pioneering discoveries and designs. But, generally, the massive forward impetus of the computer industry since the 1940s, when the first electromechanical digital computers were invented, has been engineered by large numbers of talented people working for a salary as employees of large high-tech organisations.

The extent to which pioneering technological developments are customer-centric, at least at first, is interesting. I think very likely in the early days a new kind of technology isn't necessarily customer-centric. Instead, it tends to be developed because of the inventor's or (as many new technologies have several fathers and mothers) inventors' inherent fascination with the technology.

But this inherent fascination only goes so far. If a new technology is really to get going, it needs to find, pretty soon, an application that will win the heads, hearts – and wallets – of customers.

Take the hovercraft, for example. It's an inspired idea that has never really caught on in a big way. The problem is that hovercraft are not fast enough to establish any significant advantage over automobiles, and on sea, while they are faster than boats, they are not enormously faster, nor indeed are they faster at all than fast boats such as jetfoils. Hovercraft are also extremely noisy and expensive to run, partly because containing the air cushion is difficult.

Historically, the Victorians placed great hopes in a pneumatic railway, where – believe it or not – the trains were shot along the line by means of drive pins that fitted inside a long leather tube from which the air was evacuated so that the air pressure moved the pin and thus the trains. Amazingly, this worked, but it was all very cumbersome and inefficient. Also, rats gnawed at the leather.

Technology starts out being an interesting curiosity, but in due course it really does need to earn its living by being sold to customers.

When it does, it can, of course, transform the world.

Even our inheritance as citizens of – as far as we know at present – the only high-tech world in the entire universe, is entirely dependent on the vast infrastructure of advanced technology that gives us the artefacts of this high-tech world. Take your fully-charged laptop and your mobile phone back in time to the days of Richard Arkwright, and see how utterly useless they are once their charge runs out. (I don't recommend you showing your laptop or mobile phone around, by the way; you might end up being burnt as a witch.)

The point is: the human world is built for us, *by others*, and we are utterly dependent on it for the way we live now.

But there's something else to say, too, something that has enormous implications for customer-centricity. It's this: *the human world is, generally, created and built for us by people who don't have any inherent reason to care about us personally.*

Of course, there are exceptions, such as when, for example, a friend, relative or a supplier you know builds you a conservatory or makes something else for you, or provides something.

But generally, yes, the people who make the things that you use in your life don't have any inherent reason to care about you personally. If they do care about you personally, it's only because they've taken the trouble to do so.

Also, my statement above that *the human world is, generally, created and built for us by people who don't have any inherent reason to care about us personally* obviously becomes truer as time passes.

Whatever the nature of the original relationship between supplier and customer, as time passes the nature of that original relationship will be completely forgotten, and then the owner or user of whatever has been made in the past really *will* be a complete stranger to the supplier, even to the extent that the supplier (if he or she is still alive) will not even *know* who the owner or user is. Neither, in most cases, will the customer know who the original supplier was.

If, for example, you live in a house that was not new when you bought it, you may not know who the builder was, and if your house is more than about 50 years old, the natural likelihood is that many of the people who built it will no longer be alive.

As for the other houses, schools, offices, universities, houses, shops, bus stations, railway-stations, airports – and the things all these different types of buildings contain – all of which you see in your daily life, you will very likely have little idea which individuals made them. With the passing of time, practically *everything* is seen as being made by strangers for strangers, and as more time passes *everything* is seen in this way.

When we see great buildings like St Paul's Cathedral, Westminster Abbey, the Eiffel Tower, the Colosseum, the Sistine Chapel, the Empire State Building, we know nothing about the individual people who built them, though we may know something about their architects. But the real work of actually constructing the buildings was done by people who in most cases have been dead for a long time. They never knew you, and yet you can enjoy their work long after they are dust.

As for the human world, it's *all* created by work. Look around at it. Look at the houses, the roads, the vehicles, the shops, the offices, the schools, the universities, the bus stations, the railway-stations, the airports and everything the houses, schools, offices, universities, houses, shops, bus stations, railway-stations, airports and everything else contain.

All of it, all the human world, is built by *work,* and indeed in the vast majority of cases by people you don't know and who don't know you, and never will. If they *hadn't* cared about your agenda, even though they never knew you, what they built for you would never have been built. Likewise, most of the work *we* carry out is carried out for the strangers who are so often the end-users of the work we carry out even if we know the customers who actually buy the things. This book is an obvious example: I am writing it in essence for Nick, my publisher, but my real customer is *you,* and you and I may never meet, though I hope we do.

It follows that in a world built for us by strangers, we *need* to care about the agenda of those strangers with whom we come into contact in our professional and personal lives.

Why the customer-centricity mindset requires sincerity above all

I mentioned the importance of sincerity in my Preface, when we first met, but I want to emphasise it again as the key-note of this chapter.

You can't feign the customer-centricity mindset. Either you care sincerely about what matters to all the customers you have in the different areas of your life, *or you can find the inspiration within yourself to care sincerely about this,* or you don't.

If you don't genuinely care about your customers' agenda, the chances are that you're seriously limiting the potential success of your life, both in the professional and personal spheres. Even if you already *do* care sincerely about your customers' agenda, the chances are that you could probably care *more* about it.

And even if you *do* genuinely care about your customers' agenda, but don't do anything practical to *help your customers advance their agenda*, that's pretty well as bad as not caring about your customers' agenda in the first place.

This chapter is designed to help get you into the customer-centricity mindset, or if you're already into it, which obviously I hope is the case, to make you *even more* into it. The chapter also contains material that you might wish to use, or to adapt, to help others – including your colleagues or people who report to you – to become more customer-centric.

Also, this chapter is designed to remind you why *being* in the customer-centricity mindset, is so great for your career, you personal life, and for your enjoyment of life generally. We all need reminding of this sometimes, because even the most customer-centricity-minded of us can, when we're working too hard or under too many pressures, allow ourselves to forget how important the customer-centricity mindset is.

In fact, the first beneficiary of you being in the customer-centricity mindset is you.

In a very real sense, you yourself are your most important customer.

Life and us

What do we want from life? Many of the things we want are so universally desired by human beings that it's almost banal to set down what they are: except that I think a book like this should explain its assumptions from first principles. So... I'll assume that the main things you want from life will include:

- good health, so that you can enjoy life without being constantly obliged to make compromises in your enjoyment, or to place constraints on what you do
- accommodation you enjoy in an area where you like to live
- enough money so that you can buy the things that you perceive yourself as needing, and so that you can do everything in life that you want to do, and with (ideally) ample reserves left over
- personal emotional and sexual gratification
- the happiness and health of the people who are dear to you
- an occupation you find interesting and engaging, and ideally lucrative too; if you need to earn money from your work
- a faith that you find important to yourself, whether a religious faith or a faith that originates elsewhere.

Overall, these aspects of what you want from life can, perhaps, all be summarised under this overall and perhaps most important desire of all, your desire to *feel good about yourself*.

As you know, the thinking I set down in this book is *not* only directed at people pursuing careers; the thinking is holistic in the best sense of the word, and applies to all aspects of your life. It's true that the thinking in the book is especially directed at professional and business life, but I am convinced that the ideas are relevant to all areas of your life.

In essence, my aim in this book overall, and especially in this chapter, is simple and fearless. I plan to show how you can, other things being equal, improve all aspects of your life that matter to you by adopting the thinking and the *feeling* I set down in this book, and which I describe here, in this chapter that focuses on it primarily, as the customer-centricity mindset.

I really do believe that if you follow the guidance I offer, every aspect of your life – your health; where you live; your financial position; your personal emotional and sexual life; and lastly but certainly not least, your work life – will all benefit.

If you've seen the 1983 John Landis film *Trading Places*, you'll recall the scene where Billy Ray Valentine (Eddie Murphy) is plucked pretty literally from the gutter by two ultra-wealthy and self-indulgent brothers who are debating nature versus nurture and who want to find a practical example of a person who will let them put their theories into action, and settle a financially trivial bet they have made with each other.

Having first destroyed the career of the priggish, self-centred but undoubtedly hard-working head of their commodities trading firm, they install Billy Ray there instead. Finding that the new recruit achieves rapid success in his new role, the brother who advocated nature rather than nurture ruefully remarks to Valentine that the firm did manage to stay in business for forty years before he came along.

I realise you might feel much the same: that you've managed to live your life for however long you have *without* having read this book about the customer-centricity mindset, so why should the book be such a big deal to you?

I think there are two reasons:

1. *The right kind of book can offer an extremely useful short-cut to learning important lessons about life that might otherwise take close to an entire life to learn.* Having to learn the lessons in the real world of life can not only be a painstaking process, but the lessons will very likely only be learned at great practical and emotional cost.

2. *The advice in this book works.* As an individual I have had three very different phases in my professional life. I was seventeen years old when I was accepted on a pilot training course and I worked in aviation – as a pilot, instructor and general manager of an aviation company – until I was twenty-three.

I enjoyed working in aviation, but I felt strongly that I wanted to be more involved in commerce and so I changed careers completely and began working on the shop floor for the John Lewis Partnership, selling personal computers.

I worked for the Partnership for a total of fifteen years, interrupted by a return to the world of aviation for three years. When I left the John Lewis Partnership I was a development manager for the research and expansion department. I directly managed the introduction of a customer information system that covered all the customers of John Lewis and Waitrose. I also managed the initial planning and development of John Lewis's and Waitrose's pioneering e-commerce and online sales system.

Through this work for the John Lewis Partnership I got to know the business and information technology consultancy Charteris and I joined them in October 2000. At Charteris I now head the business consulting practice.

So I have had three very different careers, but what has been absolutely and fundamentally core to all of them is my personal passion for finding out about and meeting the agenda of customers and the simple fact that I get a real buzz and excitement out of aligning an organisation to meet customer needs. I am certain that my constant focus on the customer has been a vital underpinning for all my professional life. This is the reason why I so passionately want to share my passion for customers in this book.

Can a book, in any case, help you to get into the customer-centricity mindset? Well, yes. I personally very much believe in the potential of the right kind of book to have a major, even revolutionary, on people's lives.

From the very start of this book, I've been postponing addressing the question of what kind of book *The Customer-Centric You* really *is*.

I thought it best, first, to plunge ahead with everything I wanted to say about the need to focus on the customer itself.

In fact, when I first planned *The Customer-Centric You*, I planned to make this chapter, Chapter 5, the first chapter. But as the ideas in the book began to gather momentum, it became clear to me that this chapter about the customer-centricity mindset belonged some way down the line, after the book had explored customer-centricity from a variety of perspectives.

But now it's time to think a little more about what kind of book this is. In particular, is it a self-help book or a business book? Certainly, my concept of it started out as seeing it as a business book, but in a way I can't help feeling, and I wonder whether you feel the same, that during the writing of this book it's somehow started turning itself into a self-help book by a sort of automatic process.

If this has happened, and indeed it may have done, perhaps the reason is that the nature of the material demands the self-help treatment.

So maybe I really am writing a self-help book.

Which – I admit – is a rather terrifying thing to realise.

Not because self-help books abound (though they do), but rather because there are some self-help books that have transformed life for millions of people; books that have become legendary. This being so, I am conscious of writing in exalted company.

Still, we achieve nothing by being excessively in awe of what we're trying to do, and besides, there's every reason to be proud of having a chance to produce a self-help book.

The best self-help books provide information that is not found readily anywhere else, except perhaps on the lips of knowledgeable friends or wise relatives. Except that... we're never likely to forget that advice provided by friends or relatives comes with some agenda of its own, and this is obviously not the same with a self-help book, which simply provides you with advice as part of the deal when you buy it.

It's generally true that self-help books as a major publishing phenomenon date from the early part of the twentieth century, when several factors – including the growth of a true mass market for book publishing, a new frankness in speaking about personal matters, and greater urbanisation and mobility leading to people interacting with far more people than had ever been the case in the past – conspired to make books that offered hard-hitting and pithy advice about dealing with life an attractive proposition both the publishers and readers.

However, this is not to say that no self-help books were published before the start of the twentieth century. Self-improvement books appeared during the nineteenth century too. Some talked down to readers, sometimes to a preposterous extent, and generally the tone of the books was dry and learned. But some of the books were gems, too, notably Samuel Smiles' book, actually called *Self-Help*, published in 1862. This book is largely forgotten today, but if you can get hold of a copy I very much recommend it. The very first paragraph applies rather wonderfully to the need to acquire the customer-centricity mindset.

> *'Heaven helps those who help themselves' is a well-tried maxim, embodying in small compass the results of vast human experience. The spirit of self-help is the root of all genuine growth in the individual; and, exhibited in the lives of many, it constitutes the true source of national vigour and strength. Help from without [i.e. outside] is often enfeebling in its effect, but help from within invariably invigorates. Whatever is done for men or classes, to a certain extent takes away the stimulus and necessity of doing it for themselves; and where men are subjected to over-guidance and over-government, the inevitable tendency is to render them comparatively helpless.*

In other words, applied to our subject-matter, people need to take upon themselves their own responsibility for acquiring the customer-centricity mindset; rather than expecting others to be customer-centric *for* them.

Journals in the nineteenth century often contained articles that offered advice about self-improvement. For example, the following extract comes from an article that in the 1893 annual edition of Cassell's *Family Magazine*. The extract, which begins from the start of the article, contains a little under a half of the text of the article, which as you see, had a rather hectoring tone, though the advice is sound enough:

> *Is it an art, or but a persistent attention to one duty in life? Still, to every earnest young man or woman launching out of the home circle, and especially to those intending to devote themselves to professional or commercial pursuits, the same question always presents itself: 'How am I to get on in the career I have chosen?'*
>
> *In whatever station, a constant and steady application of*

one's duty, to one's neighbour, one's employer, and one's-self, at once presents itself as the golden rule, 'How to get on,' not only with the world, but with self-content and comfort. If this rule be followed conscientiously, material welfare may not immediately result, but ease and happiness will.

The first departure from it becomes the first step on the downward road to failure, and fortunate indeed will it be if simple failure in getting on be the only result. A few trite maxims, with instances of their application, or want of application, present themselves as the readiest guides to the golden rule referred to, and many of them will be applicable both to domestic and business life. But let us confine ourselves first to the business aspect of the question, and, supposing our beginner just launched in a career, give some guides for future conduct.

Be punctual. A stoppage for 'lost time' or a fine for late attendance will not condone the fault or remove the bad impression given to those employing you. You may be a very small cog in the business wheel, but the cog, however small, must always be in its place. Many a train has been lost by a master owing to the absence of the lad who should have carried the parcel to it.

Carry out your orders implicitly, even if you think your master is making a mistake, and execute them to the best of your ability. Your master must be supposed to know his business best, and if he has been wrong, your time has been of less importance than his, and he will think better of you for having made the trial. On the other hand, if the work had been done your way, and turned out wrong, the irritating excuse, 'But I thought,' would soon have been found to make matters worse.

Don't be impatient when shown you are wrong, or when you are told how to do a thing, even if you think you know. Nothing wearies a superior more than the exhibition of feeling, whether expressed in manner or by the petulant 'Oh, bother!' of young people. 'I know' soon gets let alone, and either remains untaught, or, like Little Uzbec, in 'Tales of the Sixty Mandarins,' has to learn by bitter experience.

Always keep your temper, even if unjustly accused, and be civil both to those above and beneath you. 'A soft answer turneth away wrath,' and silence with an angry employer is best, for you can justify yourself in calmer moments. Such an instance occurred recently in an accountant's office, when the principal accused a clerk of causing a heavy loss by not attending to orders. In the heat of the moment a denial would have been followed by dismissal, but two days after a modest presentation of the principal's memorandum (from which the order was omitted) not only brought an apology, but was the prelude to promotion.

Don't be above your work, or mind doing little things – they are steps to something greater. It is an every-day occurrence in large offices for juniors to be passed over when vacancies happen with the remark, 'He does not do his present work properly, and cannot, therefore be trusted with better.' It is not often that a false pride has been conquered in the amusing manner in which a manager cured a junior clerk, who, on being asked to take a bundle of papers to another office, responded: 'He had not been engaged to carry parcels.' Instead of dismissing him for his impertinence, the manager said, 'Oh get your hat and come with me;' and the lad, to his dismay, found himself walking up the street by the side of his superior, who himself carried the parcel. The lesson went home, and it was not long before the culprit was begging to be allowed to take the package.

Don't be afraid of trouble – what is worth doing at all is worth doing well. The temptation to 'scamp' work in order to get it over or to find time to play is very common but its effect is always disastrous. Even if you do not obtain a character as a careless workman, the habit will speedily grow to an extent which will prevent your being able to do good work, even when so disposed. 'It's not worth while to take the trouble,' or 'What is the good?' are both sayings far too common – they are indications of a lazy mind, and their exponents never get on.

That last paragraph of advice is, of course, especially relevant to customer-centricity.

Let's now fast-forward into the 1930s, and take a look at a particular self-help book that is itself, without consciously setting out to be, profoundly a book about how to become more customer-centric. I've mentioned the book before – Dale Carnegie's *How To Win Friends and Influence People* – now it's time to look at in more detail.

Dale Carnegie and his beliefs

How To Win Friends and Influence People was the most successful self-help book of the twentieth century. The book was published in 1936, during the difficult years of economic depression and political instability that had their terrible culmination in World War Two. The very fact of *How To Win Friends and Influence People* being published in the free world, just three years before war broke out, seems to me to be indicative of something profoundly important about that free world, and the values that free world enshrined and which it fought for so hard. One can hardly imagine a book with the title *How To Win Friends and Influence People* being published in Nazi Germany, and in fact there was indeed no German-language edition of this book published under the Nazis. Surprise, surprise.

How To Win Friends and Influence People has never been out of print, though the more recent editions have been revised somewhat compared with the first version.

Carnegie was born in 1888, in poverty, on a farm in Missouri. When he was born his surname was actually 'Carnegey'; he changed the spelling of his surname in 1922, apparently deliberately so that the spelling of his surname would be that of great Scottish-born American industrialist Andrew Carnegie, who was one of Dale's personal heroes.

At school and college Dale Carnegie was active in debating clubs. When he graduated from college he worked first as a salesman in Nebraska, then as an actor in New York and finally he began teaching public speaking while he was living in the YMCA on New York's 125th Street. Having decided he would like to teach public speaking, Carnegie persuaded the YMCA's manager to let him teach a class in return for eighty percent of the net proceeds.

During his first teaching session, Carnegie – having run out of material – found himself forced to improvise. He had the brainwave of suggesting to his students that they should speak about 'something that made them angry'. Right away Carnegie found that this technique made people unafraid to address a public audience.

When Carnegie began this phase of his career he was aware of having found his vocation. His classes in New York became enormously popular, and he was soon lecturing to packed houses not only about public speaking, but also about general matters relating to how his students presented themselves to the world and related to other people.

From the outset, Carnegie's advice was practical; the kind of advice that could be learned in the morning and put into practice over lunch. Not that this is in any way to belittle the nature of his advice; indeed, its ready usefulness is one of its most powerful plus points.

Carnegie's teaching preached the importance of the right kind of personal attitude, of *genuine* (as opposed to feigned) regard for and respect for others, of honesty and a willingness to admit one was wrong if one is. His thinking also embodied the important principle – which at heart seems obvious but had never been properly articulated before and incorporated into practical guidance – that it is possible to change the behaviour of others if we change how we treat *them*.

This point, *that we can through our own efforts effect an improvement in the way the world is towards us*, is an enormously important insight in anyone's life. It is all very well to say that the lesson is obvious, but if it *is* so obvious, why are most people so bad at implementing it?

Carnegie's articulate and entertaining articulation of the idea seemed positively revolutionary in the rapacious, merciless economic world of the 1930s where (unlike the developed world today) you could starve if you failed in your career.

Today, in a more liberated, probably generally happier and certainly more self-aware society than the one of the United States in the 1930s, the lesson is no less momentous.

From the point of view of *The Customer-Centric You*, what it is vital to point out is that the *core* of Carnegie's advice counsels, above all, against going through life utterly preoccupied with one's own agenda while remaining indifferent, or at best merely slavishly respectful, to the agenda of others.

Carnegie preaches the need actively to seek to develop an interest in others and not to be too haughty about oneself.

In his general teaching, Carnegie liked to remind people, especially when they began to be successful, that they should not become so proud that they forgot that there were only who they were by an accident of fate. 'Remember,' he would say, '*the only reason you are not a rattlesnake is that your parents were not rattlesnakes.*'

Which is, I think, excellent advice, for it tends to instil a fundamental humility in oneself, and no-one who does not have some humility is likely to be very good at listening to customers and what they want.

Another way of looking at Carnegie's advice is to reflect that we are only who we are due to the fortunate fact of having been born a member of a species that has taken about four billion years to evolve. Even if you'd instead been born three million years ago – which is only yesterday compared to the vast stretch of time since life on earth first evolved – you'd have been a four-foot tall man-ape *Australopithecus*, and your life would have been very different from today. You certainly wouldn't be reading this book, for one thing. Let's therefore be glad we were born when we were, and let's use our natures as human beings to make the most of ourselves and to do what we can in the world, too.

Carnegie didn't distinguish between advice relating to one's business life or one's personal life; it was all the same to him: indeed, he actively promoted the idea that one should in effect be the person one was in all walks of life: not just have a business persona and a personal persona.

Given the popularity of Carnegie's lectures, it isn't surprising that his work were soon packaged into book form. A publishing executive named Leon Shimkin, who worked with the US publisher

Simon & Schuster, took one of the 14-week courses given by Carnegie in 1934. Shimkin persuaded Carnegie to allow a stenographer to take notes from the course and for the notes to be revised for publication. The resulting book was in its 17th printing within a few months of its first publication. By the time of Carnegie's death in 1955 at the age of 66, the book had sold five million copies and since then has sold another ten million.

How To Win Friends and Influence People is an easy read – yet also a fascinating, provocative and extremely engaging one. The format consists of relatively short chapters that teach a particular principle, usually through a combination of inspirational writing and pithy anecdote. In essence, the book highlights certain key aspects of human social psychology and explains how you can put these into action *in an uncynical, genuine way* in your own life.

This is a crucial point: Carnegie always counsels sincerity. The book emphasises not only that the individual's personal attitude is crucial, but that, in fact, *it's actually quite easy to change one's attitude if one really wants to.*

This is another vital point. A tragically large number of people go through life achieving next to nothing, and causing little but grief and anguish to those with whom they interact in a professional and personal capacity, simply due to stubbornness and an unwillingness to change who they are.

Why are they like this? Why are they reluctant to change? Why do they take such a pride in being who they are, even when who they are is pretty lousy? Why are they so willing to give voice to that banal mantra of the eternally unsuccessful: *I am who I am?*

I'm not a psychologist, and so I don't know why so many people are like that, and like to say that, but I do know that no-one who is unprepared to question their introspection, or to think of how they can be better to others and to the world, or how they can be better at what they do professionally, is likely to make much of their life.

So often, an unpleasant attitude stemming from just one person can ruin families, destroy relationships, and sow the seeds of unhappiness and personal trauma that can reverberate down the decades.

Of course, this is all true in terms of the wrong attitude at a political level as well as in a personal sense. No matter how abominable one regards the behaviour of the Nazi party in Germany in the decade before World War Two and in the War itself, even this scale of evil had to be spawned somewhere. Few historians today would doubt that if the victorious powers, at the end of the First World War, had not been so vindictive towards Germany in the terms of the Versailles Settlement, Germany most likely would not in the next twenty years have been reduced to the abject poverty that gave Hitler and his cronies the opportunity to convince decent Germans that rule by the Nazis could only be an improvement on the way life was.

The victorious powers after World War I thought they were being right in punishing Germany by imposing a draconian reparations bill on Germany. What they forgot is that a country is not a person, and that if a country is punished economically it is going to be the poorest people in the country – who may be completely innocent of any involvement in the behaviour for which the country is being punished – who will suffer the most. And so Germany became comprehensively impoverished, which was a major contributing factor to the events that led to World War II.

Fortunately, after *that* war, the victorious allies had the sense to help Germany economically (especially the part that became West Germany), and helped to create the conditions in Germany for the 'Economic Miracle' that led to Germany becoming a wealthy and passionate advocate of peace in Europe and in the world. True, the allies may have done what they did mainly to stop West Germany falling under Soviet influence, but the positive effect upon West Germany was undeniable.

Ultimately, what finished off communism as practised in the Soviet Union what that it didn't bring its citizens the consumer goods they wanted. In the end, communism wasn't sufficiently customer-centric.

For the victorious allies, having an attitude towards Germany conducive to Germany's prosperity was absolutely vital in creating the conditions that have brought peace to most of Europe since 1945.

In customer-centricity, as in power politics, the right attitude is essential.

The point is, focusing on the attitude of the individual is *not* trivial. On the contrary, it is major, and by far the most important thing on which one *should* focus. The trouble is, by and large most people are more interested in being right than in being constructive.

Within an organisation that is not currently infused with customer-centricity, it is perfectly possible that a principal cause of the organisation's lack of customer-centricity is that too many people working there feel that their perception that they are 'right' in how they are towards customers is, in fact, more important than the organisation actually *being* customer-centric. Such people are, of course, long overdue for a harsh dose of reality.

But indeed it is true that too more people, both within organisations and in the world generally, fail to question their own introspection sufficiently and spend too much energy in wanting to be right rather than in wanting to do a good job for their customers or for other people generally.

Such people are dangerous in all areas of life, and pose special dangers within an organisation seeking to become more customer-centric *because they are likely to be against change*, and an organisation that is not currently customer-centric absolutely must change if the organisation is to have any chance of becoming customer-centric.

But – and here's the really exciting news – in the right circumstances, and with the correct kind of guidance, people can soon be taught and encouraged to improve their attitude and the quality of their customer-related thinking generally, and can be made to be advocates of customer-centricity.

How To Win Friends and Influence People caught the spirit of its time and won millions of readers. The book's anecdotes that drive the book's lessons home have a pithy simplicity about them.

One of many highly instructive anecdotes in the book concerns Dale Carnegie's namesake, Andrew Carnegie. In a chapter designed to teach readers that the most important sound in the world to anyone is the sound of their own name, Dale Carnegie explains that

Andrew Carnegie (who was known as the Steel King) learned this lesson while still only a boy and practised it all his life. Dale Carnegie writes that later in Andrew Carnegie's career, he and the railway magnate George Pullman were fighting for supremacy in the railway sleeping-card business. Andrew Carnegie met with Pullman in a New York hotel and proposed that instead of slugging things out they should merge their interests and create a new corporation and work together. Pullman listened but was not convinced. He asked Andrew Carnegie what the new organisation would be called. Carnegie replied at once that it would be called the Pullman Palace Car Company.

George Pullman lost his hesitation at once. In the mid-to-late nineteenth century through the early decades of the twentieth century, the Pullman Palace Car Company was a major manufacturer of railway rolling stock, as well as of streetcars and trolley-buses.

There have been other successful self-help books since *How To Win Friends and Influence People* was published, but none of these has quite had the impact of Dale Carnegie's, possibly because he had so much to say, and what he was saying was so overdue in needing to be said.

Yes, as we've already seen that Carnegie was not a pioneer in the self-help genre. Nor was he, for all his wonderful and perceptive emphasis on the need to pay genuine and truly attentive interest in the agenda of strangers, a pioneer in saying that. He had been beaten to the post some decades earlier, by one of the greatest Victorian writers, Charles Dickens.

Charles Dickens – customer-centricity guru

We've already seen that the novelist Charles Dickens was highly customer-centric because he knew what his readers wanted, both in terms of the content of his work and the regularly serialised form in which it was published.

Dickens also promoted, in his writings and general outlook on life, a philosophy of life based on the need to care about and empathise with the agenda of others. It is known from his own private conversations and from his letters that his philosophy in this respect was something he cherished and took care not only to embody in his work, but also to teach his children and emphasise to his friends.

In his novel *David Copperfield* (1850) for example, Dickens describes two schools that the young David attends. One, run by a Mr Creakle, whose favourite teaching aid is the cane, is portrayed as a nightmarish place where terrified boys learn next to nothing. Another school whose headmaster is a benevolent gentleman called Dr Strong, is a well-run, kindly place where the boys love to learn. Dickens, writing as David Copperfield, compares the schools.

> *Doctor Strong's was an excellent school,* **as different from Mr Creakle's as good is from evil.*** *It was very gravely and decorously ordered, and on a sound system; with an appeal, in everything, to the honour and good faith of the boys... which worked wonders. We all felt that we had a part in the management of the place, and in sustaining its character and dignity. Hence, we soon became warmly attached to it − I am sure I did for one, and I never knew, in all my time, of any boy being otherwise − and learnt with a good will, desiring to do it credit. We had noble games out of hours, and plenty of liberty, but even then, as I remember, we were well spoken of in the town, and rarely did any disgrace, by our appearance or manner, to the reputation of Doctor Strong and Doctor Strong's boys. (*My bold highlighting)*

I highlight the phrase *as different from Mr Creakle's as good is from evil*, because that really is the point: Dickens *does* regard a good internal attitude as being as different from a bad attitude as good is from evil.

The above passage from *David Copperfield* is quoted in an entertaining and perceptive article about Dickens by George Orwell that Orwell wrote in 1939. Referring to this passage about the two schools, Orwell says:

In the woolly vagueness of this passage one can see Dickens's utter lack of any educational theory. He can imagine the moral atmosphere of a good school, but nothing further. The boys 'learnt with a good will' but what did they learn?

Of course, at one level Orwell is right, except that Dickens is a novelist – that is, a historian of society who *shows* us what life is rather than only *tells* us – and not an educational theorist. For Dickens, the moral atmosphere of the two schools *is* what matters, and this is why Dickens's work is so relevant, indeed red-hot relevant, to *The Customer-Centric You*.

The point is this: what Dickens is saying is that *personal internal attitude is what matters*, because if the entity is an individual this will obviously be the case, and if the entity is some other kind of organisation, its internal attitude will, of course, be determined by the attitude of the people managing it and working within it and with whom outsiders, such as customers, interact.

Ultimately what Dickens is saying is, given only a slightly different cast, what I'm saying here in *The Customer-Centric You*: namely, that the customer-centricity mindset *is* indeed about personal attitude, about a genuine and sincere willingness to be interested in the customer's agenda and to act on that interest to take every step to bring to customers what they want.

George Orwell, in his essay on Dickens about the passage in *David Copperfield* about the difference between Mr Creakle's school and Doctor Strong's, has this to say.

It seems that in every attack Dickens makes upon society he is always pointing to a change of spirit rather than a change of structure. It is hopeless to try and pin him down to any definite remedy, still more to anyone political doctrine. His approach is always along the moral plane, and his attitude is sufficiently summed up in that remark about Strong's school being as different from a Creakle's 'as good is from evil'. Two things can be very much alike and yet abysmally different. Heaven and hell are in the same place. Useless to changes institutions without a 'change of heart' – that, essentially, is what he is saying.

This whole paragraph is enormously important for thinking about the customer-centricity mindset.

Yes, a change of spirit rather than a change of structure *is* what matters and indeed what is called for. An organisation that is more preoccupied with its own stuff than with its customers *does* need a change of spirit, a change of internal attitude, and indeed it needs this very badly. It may also need a change of structure to ensure that its processes are aligned with its new customer-friendly mindset, but this chapter is about mindset rather than processes.

Yes, two things can indeed be very much alike and yet utterly different. Heaven and hell really can be in the same place; *it all depends on the attitude and the governing sensibility that prevail there.* To apply this thinking in an example from the business world, a call centre that cares about its customers and really focuses on them rather than purely on its own agenda is a call centre made in heaven; one that sees customers as nuisances is one made in hell.

Paul Crampton, at the start of his novel *Ronnie Darwin Was My Uncle* (2006), paints an all-too-plausible picture of life in such a call centre: one that is set up by a large telecoms utility to deal with incoming customer queries and complaints:

> *08:59, on a Monday morning, was by far the most daunting and depressing time of the whole week, thought Dave Darwin with dread, as the seconds counted down to the time when the telephone switchboard opened up.*
>
> *'Stand by your beds!' yelled someone keenly, from the opposite end of the office, almost as if that person relished the prospect.*
>
> *Dave watched the second hand jerking round to the hour, and just knew that of all the people in his immediate block of four desks, his own phone would be the first to ring.*
>
> *'We're open for business!' enthused the same motivated madman from the far end, as an unseen button was pressed to start the day's business going.*

Dave does his best, but the whole culture of the telecoms service provider that employs him is designed to deal with customers as quickly and peremptorily as possible: customers are seen in this call centre as little more than a nuisance.

This call centre example, as much as the literary example of the two schools that David Copperfield attends and George Orwell's comments on the passage in which Dickens compares the two schools, emphasises a vital point.

This point is that *internal attitude – generated by the people with the power to bring change to the entity in question and also generated by the people who liaise directly with customers – is what matters*. Internal attitude, indeed, may boil down to the attitude of just a few people, the people at the top of an organisation, the people who have the power to influence everyone else there and the charisma to make their influence inspirational, which is the best kind of influence.

In truth, internal attitude may boil down to the attitude of just one person. I don't like mentioning the Nazis, still less Hitler, but imagine if Hitler had had the sense to see the enormous contribution German Jews had made to Germany's business life, professional life and culture... and the similar contribution made by Jewish people in other countries. The entire history of the Jewish people since the 1930s would have been different, and the world would have been blessed, today, with millions of descendants of Jews murdered in the holocaust, descendants who were never born because of the unspeakable wickedness of the Nazis.

So please don't think that internal attitude, personal attitude, isn't the basis of everything. It is.

Heaven and hell in the same place? Potentially, yes. A Germany led by an enlightened Hitler who saw German Jews and other Jewish people as colleagues would have been heaven compared with the hell that was Nazi Germany.

We human beings had better get personal attitude right, too. A great deal more than customer relationships is at stake, though that certainly *is* at stake. If we human beings can't learn to empathise with one another and care about one another, we may either end up wiping ourselves out, or even if we don't do that, we may eventually cease to flourish as a species and wind up being replaced as the dominant species on this planet by some other species that's more empathetic, more customer-friendly, more cheerful, and in the final analysis just plain nicer.

On a lighter note, there's a joke that I think helps to sum up much of the above discussion. It's a joke about a writer.

A writer dies after a long life of honest, hard toil and is delighted to find that he (or she, but for grammatical simplicity we'll make him male in this case) has been selected to go to heaven. He ascends a golden staircase, enters the pearly gates and meets St Peter, who welcomes him and shows him round heaven, which turns out to consist of a huge room like a ballroom, with exquisite wood panelling and wood carvings, and with real-life seraphim and cherubim flying around the ceiling.

The room is filled with dozens of desks, at which writers are working hard at their word-processors on their latest books.

'Great!' exclaims the recently deceased writer. 'I'm really going to feel at home here. Writing's what I love to do and now I can write for all eternity!'

'I am glad, my son, that you are happy with your just reward for all your labours,' replies St Peter.

'Thanks again,' says the ecstatic writer. 'I just have one question; sorry, like all writers I'm a bit too inquisitive for my own good. I wonder what hell's like?'

'No problem, my son,' St Peter returns. 'Follow me and I'll show you.'

So the writer follows St Peter out through the pearly gates, and down the golden staircase and along a corridor that, St Peter explains, leads to hell.

The writer is expecting the smell of brimstone and to hear the wails of the eternally condemned, but instead Peter presently leads him into a room that looks *exactly* like the one in heaven. It's a huge room, with exquisite wood panelling and wood carving, and with real-life seraphim and cherubim flying around the ceiling. Just as in heaven, the room is filled with dozens of desks, at which writers are working hard at their word-processors on their latest books.

The writer, astonished, turns to St Peter. 'I'm sorry, I just don't understand it. Am I back in heaven again?'

'No, my son, believe me, this is hell.'

'But it can't be!' the writer protests, 'it's just like heaven!'

'Not at all, my son,' St Peter replies. 'This truly is hell. You see, in heaven, *the books get published.*'

It's a joke with a serious point: in heaven the writers are customer-centric: they're published because they know how to give the reading public – their customers – what they want. Let's remember what Orwell said about heaven and hell being in the same place. In this joke, outwardly, they *are*, just as an organisation that is in the heavenly state of being fully customer-centric may not look *too* different, outwardly, from one in the hellish situation of not being customer-centric at all.

Believe me, whether all writers will find this joke funny I can't tell you, but they'll certainly all agree about what constitutes the difference between heaven and hell as far as writers are concerned.

All of Charles Dickens's work amounts to a giant contribution to the theme – so central to us here in our thinking about customer-centricity – of *true and sincere empathy with others.*

One of the clearest and most concise expressions of this theme is found in his remarkable short novel *A Christmas Carol,* which wonderfully, and with unforgettable dramatic passion and conviction, argues that we can only find salvation as human creatures by caring about and empathising with our fellow-humans and expressing that care and empathy in heartfelt deeds.

Dickens himself was profoundly aware of the importance of the philosophy expounded in *A Christmas Carol,* and indeed he often referred to this attitude to life as 'Carol-philosophy', referring directly to the world-famous masterpiece in which the philosophy is dramatised with such complete success.

In its own way, *A Christmas Carol* is as vitally important for anyone who wants to think about customers in the way they should properly be thought about, as *How To Win Friends and Influence People* or indeed any other great self-help book.

A Christmas Carol is a moral fable about the joy, fulfilment and sheer happiness that fills our lives if we can start to care genuinely about the agenda of others.

The story, by the way, is far more interesting and subtle in its original form as the Dickens novella, rather than in the often sentimental, clumsily updated or even absurd movie versions emitted by Hollywood on an almost annual basis.

The tale, which Dickens wrote over about six weeks in the late autumn of 1843, finishing it in the first week of December in time for publication by Christmas, begins on a dark, foggy Christmas Eve afternoon. We meet Ebeneezer Scrooge, a successful, grasping, hard-hearted, solitary man of business (we are never told precisely what his business is) who operates from a counting-house in the City of London, aided by his one employee, an impoverished clerk called Bob Cratchit.

Scrooge's treatment of Bob is so tight-fisted that he even forbids him to add more coal to Bob's tiny fire, on pain of getting sacked. Interestingly, while Scrooge is usually portrayed in screen or theatre adaptations of the story as an elderly man in his sixties or even seventies, in Dickens's story numerical information makes clear that Scrooge is only supposed to be in his late forties or thereabouts. This is an important point: in the story, Dickens attributes Scrooge's harsh and life-hating nature to Scrooge's personality rather than to the fact of his being old.

Some modern critics regard Scrooge as a projection by Dickens of some aspects of himself: a sort of expression by Dickens of his guilt at his own success. In real life, Dickens was mostly a generous-minded and warm-hearted fellow who worked like a slave for his own customers – his readers – and took great care to give them what they wanted.

But even Dickens could be Scrooge-like on occasion; for example, he became impatient of the constant requests for money from many of the members of his family other than his own wife and children.

In another case, when the novelist Hans Christian Andersen came to stay, Dickens found the socially clumsy, child-like, virginal Danish writer a crashing bore and after Andersen went home Dickens had a card put above the mirror in the bedroom where Andersen had stayed. The card read: 'Hans Andersen slept in this room for five weeks – which seemed to the family AGES!' Later, Dickens frequently did not bother to respond to Andersen's letters.

Clearly, even the most customer-centric of us have moods and times when we do not feel inclined to be warm to people. Of course, we need to understand these moods and prevent them from influencing our behaviour. Indeed, perhaps one way of reading *A Christmas Carol*, is to see it as being about the life of anyone who is passionately attached to work that is by its nature largely solitary, with Dickens depicting solitary work as robbing the person of the delights of true contact with their fellow human beings, until the person is induced to realise how important other human beings are. Whether Dickens himself recognised this aspect of his story is another matter, but as we've seen, subconscious was not a word, or indeed even a concept, to which he had access.

Indeed, we are *all* liable to get too immersed in our own agenda.

The whole philosophy of customer-centricity – that we need to find it in ourselves to remind ourselves constantly of the importance of the agenda of others – is in fact not only a philosophy for business, but for all life.

As for Scrooge, despite being – as Dickens puts it – 'as solitary as an oyster' – he is not completely without family. He has a nephew – the son of Scrooge's deceased sister – who visits him on Christmas Eve and is then, at the start of the story, informed by Scrooge that Christmas is nothing but 'humbug'.

Scrooge, we discover, never keeps Christmas, and when two men of his own social class come to visit him to ask him for a donation towards the welfare of the poor at Christmas-tide, Scrooge says he will give nothing, especially as the prisons, workhouses and treadmill are in 'full vigour'. On being asked by one of the gentleman whether he wishes to be anonymous, Scrooge says he wishes to be left alone, and adds:

> *'Since you ask me what I wish, gentlemen, that is my answer. I don't make merry myself at Christmas, and I can't afford to make idle people merry. I help to support the establishments I have mentioned; they cost enough: and those who are badly off must go there.'*
>
> *'Many can't go there, and many would rather die.'*
>
> *'If they would rather die,' said Scrooge, 'they had better do it, and decrease the surplus population'.*

This mention of the concept of 'surplus population' is a deeply ironic reference by Dickens to Thomas Malthus's *Essay on the Principles of Population* (1803), in which Malthus sets forth, among other things, the bizarre argument that if someone is born into a world whose land has already been allocated to other people, and if he is unable to get subsistence from his parents, and if society does not want his labour, then that person

> *has no claim of right to the smallest portion of food, and, in fact, has no business to be where he is. At nature's mighty feast there is no vacant cover for him. She tells him to be gone...*

The 'surplus population' was this proportion of the population that fitted the criteria laid down by Malthus in his ghastly condemnation of all who were not fortunate to be born into money.

Of course, this was all very well for Malthus, who did not count himself as one of those who was surplus. The idea that, in effect, a baby born without money, or without parents who will bring it up, does not deserve to live is at best sinister and at worst utterly evil, yet in the nineteenth century the ideas of Malthus were highly regarded by many (wealthy, naturally) people.

Scrooge is visited, through the good agency of his seven-years-dead former business partner Jacob Marley, by the Ghost of Christmas Past. This first spirit takes Scrooge back to his, Scrooge's, own childhood and lets Scrooge see where his cold-hearted indifference to others came from. This episode from the story is, among other things, an astonishing anticipation of modern psychology's attribution of the origin of adult characteristics to childhood experiences.

Scrooge is next visited by the Ghost of Christmas Present, who takes an invisible Scrooge to many Christmas Day parties, including the humble, impoverished but warm-hearted celebrations of Bob Cratchit and his family, including Bob's youngest child, Tiny Tim, a cripple. I think it probable that Victorian audiences would have inferred from Dickens's descriptions of the Cratchits that Tim's lameness was caused by malnutrition, and this appears to be something Dickens is suggesting (though he never refers to it explicitly) in terms of how the story develops.

> Then Bob proposed:
> 'A Merry Christmas to us all, my dears. God bless us!'
> Which all the family re-echoed.
> 'God bless us every one!' said Tiny Tim, the last of all.
> He sat very close to his father's side, on his little stool. Bob held his withered little hand in his, as if he loved the child, and wished to keep him by his side, and dreaded that he might be taken from him.
> 'Spirit,' said Scrooge, with an interest he had never felt before, 'tell me if Tiny Tim will live.'

'I see a vacant seat,' replied the ghost, 'in the poor chimney corner, and a crutch without an owner, carefully preserved. If these shadows remain unaltered by the future, the child will die.'

'No, no,' said Scrooge. 'Oh no, kind spirit, say he will be spared.'

'If these shadows remain unaltered by the future, none other of my race,' returned the ghost, 'will find him here. What then? If he be like to die, he had better do it, and decrease the surplus population.'

Scrooge hung his head to hear his own words quoted by the spirit, and was overcome with penitence and grief.

'Man,' said the ghost, 'if man you be in heart, not adamant, forbear that wicked cant until you have discovered What the surplus is, and Where it is. Will you decide what men shall live, what men shall die? It may be, that in the sight of heaven, you are more worthless and less fit to live than millions like this poor man's child.'

Scrooge's conversion springs substantially from him being forced to witness, by magical means, the true nature of humanity – with all its vulnerability and hope, and the particular plight of the young and impoverished. Dickens conveys this aspect of Scrooge's conversion with splendidly moving power.

Let's remember that this was the author who, when only 25 years told, wrote the story of Oliver Twist. Oliver's name, by the way, is a pun on 'All of a twist', which was how Dickens saw the cruel Poor Laws on his day: laws that were about as un-customer-centric as it is possible to imagine, for they scarcely provided for poor children who were in the 'care' of the parish to be given enough food to stay alive.

The final nail, so to speak, in the coffin of the old Scrooge is, literally, driven home when Scrooge is shown, by the Ghost of Christmas to Come, a vision of his own solitary death, unmourned by any. Indeed, the only consequence of Scrooge's death are the robbery of his clothes and curtain-hangings by petty thieves, and also the happiness of a young couple, in debt to him, who feel that his death may relieve the burden of their indebtedness, as – while they know that the debt will doubtless be transferred to some other creditor – 'it would be bad fortune indeed to find so merciless a creditor in his successor.'

The moral of *A Christmas Carol* is clear: live with a warm heart and a generous spirit and regard your fellow creatures as – to use the words of Scrooge's nephew – 'fellow-passengers to the grave'. Indeed, Jacob Marley's Ghost has already made plain the message that Dickens wants to convey:

Scrooge fell upon his knees, and clasped his hands before his face.

'Mercy!' he said. 'Dreadful apparition, why do you trouble me?'

'Man of the worldly mind!' replied the Ghost. 'Do you believe in me or not?'

'I do,' said Scrooge. 'I must. But why do spirits walk the earth, and why do they come to me?'

'It is required of every man,' the Ghost returned, 'that the

spirit within him should walk abroad among his fellow-men, and travel far and wide; and if that spirit goes not forth in life, it is condemned to do so after death.'

For Jacob Marley it was too late, but fortunately not for Scrooge, who wakes on Christmas Day after his three hauntings to discover that the Ghosts of Christmas Past, Present and to Come and done have all their inspirational work in just one night. Far from being dead, Scrooge has another chance, and finds that the world is his in which to make reparations and to be the man he now wants to be.

The ending of *A Christmas Carol* is sheer joy, for us as readers as much as for Scrooge. After a final scene in which Scrooge promises Bob Cratchit to raise his salary, and in which he says he will 'endeavour to assist your struggling family', Scrooge orders Bob to make up the fires and buy another coal-scuttle, and that they'll discuss Bob's affairs over a bowl of the hot fruit punch the Victorians called 'bishop.'

Concluding his story, Dickens says:

Scrooge was better than his word. He did it all, and infinitely more, and to Tiny Tim, who did NOT die, he was a second father. He became as good a friend, as good a master, as good a man, as the good old city knew, or any other good old city, town, or borough, in the good old world. Some people laughed to see the alteration in him, but he let them laugh, and little heeded them; for he was wise enough to know that nothing ever happened on this globe, for good, at which some people did not have their fill of laughter in the outset... His own heart laughed, and that was quite enough for him.

He had no further intercourse with Spirits, but lived upon the Total Abstinence Principle, ever afterwards; and it was always said of him, that he was a man who knew how to keep Christmas well, if any man alive possessed the knowledge. May that be truly said of us, and all of us! And so, as Tiny Tim observed, God bless Us, Every One!

A Christmas Carol makes us imagine, with a fearful poignancy, how dreadful it would be if Scrooge were indeed dead, and could *not* make amends. Dickens himself once remarked that all his stories were about the same thing: redemption.

Likewise, one of my messages in *this* book, *The Customer-Centric You*, is that no matter how little customer-centricity has been infused into an organisation, or an individual, in the past, the organisation or individual can be redeemed by infusing itself with customer-centricity *now.*

Frank Capra's 1946 movie *It's a Wonderful Life*, now one of the most popular movies of all time, offers an extremely interesting take on the customer-centricity theme.

George Bailey, on the face of it a comparatively ordinary American man growing up in a small town, is propelled by his sense of fair play to abandon his dreams of travelling abroad and instead to take over the leadership of his hometown's loans and mortgages company. He does this partly in order to prevent the company from falling into the hands of the town's baddie, a cold-hearted and unfeeling business magnate called Potter: a character not unlike Scrooge before his reformation. While the movie is in no way a modern version of *A Christmas Carol*, its theme – that redemption comes from friendship and caring about people and loving them – echoes Dickens's story in many places.

Bailey, driven to despair by the accidental loss of a wad of banknotes amounting to US$8,000 – perhaps nowadays worth about US$150,000 – which, unknown to him, has been picked up by Potter, is about to commit suicide. However, he is saved by a guardian angel (played by an actor who does not look like a supernatural being but rather like a chubby circus clown) who has been sent from heaven to show George Bailey what an immense contribution he has made to his town, Bedford Falls, and its people.

Bailey only realises this by being shown what life in the town would be like if he had never lived. I'd better not say too much more about the plot of the movie in case you haven't seen it. I don't want to spoil your enjoyment of it.

In effect, the movie is very much two films in one: the first hour is rather slow, somewhat inconsequential and one often feels that James Stewart (who plays Bailey) has not really got into his character properly. However, the second half of the movie is masterly, and the final quarter of an hour is unquestionably one of the most moving fifteen minutes in cinematic history. It is hard to watch the second half of the movie and keep one's eyes dry.

The message – that we are all members of the same community and had better remember that, and that, as the angel expresses it, 'no man is a failure who has friends' – doubtless had much resonance a year after the end of a global war that came close to destroying civilisation.

What has always struck me about *It's a Wonderful Life* is that George Bailey in effect discovers at the end of the movie that he has always been customer-centric without realising it!

Interestingly, *It's a Wonderful Life* was a flop when it was first released, though it did receive five Oscar nominations, but no awards. It only became popular because in the 1970s, due to an administrative slip-up, the film lost its copyright protection and could consequently by screened by any TV channel without the channel having to pay for it. The film therefore became a permanent fixture on TV screens, and indeed is often the movie seen on TVs *in* movies.

Incidentally, if you know the *Back to the Future* trilogy, you'll most likely notice that in *Back to the Future II,* the nightmarish presentation of Hill Valley when ruled by Biff the tycoon, echoes many aspects of the version of Bailey's town without Bailey's influence and called Pottersville. There is even a clear homage to *It's a Wonderful Life* in one tracking scene where the camera takes us through the nightmarish Hill Valley showing us all the unpleasant bars and gambling joints that have sprung up, just as in *It's a Wonderful Life,* where the camera takes us through the Bailey-less Pottersville showing us the dancing and drinking places that now dominate the town.

Caring about the agenda of strangers

On the face of it, the themes of *How To Win Friends and Influence People*, *A Christmas Carol* and *It's a Wonderful Life* have little in common; indeed, some might see any attempt to lump the three works together as faintly ridiculous.

But if you think about it, what *is* in fact ridiculous – and tragic – is that so many people persist, against not only the interests of other people but even against their own interests, to *have little or no inherent interest in the agenda of strangers at all, and are too blind to that agenda to realise that this indifference is generally the biggest reason why they don't fulfil themselves either professionally or in a personal sense.*

Notice I say 'the agenda of strangers'. This is vitally important. As we've seen, our world is mostly built for us by strangers, and the very nature of the creation of products and services means that once the initial transaction that led to them being bought and sold is forgotten, *everything* will seem to have been produced for us by strangers. As for the customers in our professional lives, by definition they will usually be strangers, at least to start with. Being customer-centric in our professional lives means caring about the agenda of strangers.

This is the true challenge.

This book is really mostly about empathising with the agenda of people we *don't* know. That is what being customer-centric in our lives means, and the larger an organisation becomes, and the greater the extent to which it is true, because the greater the extent to which it will need to rely on winning the hearts of customers who are initially strangers.

Remember what Marley's Ghost told Scrooge: '*It is required of every man...that the spirit within him should walk abroad among his fellow-men, and travel far and wide.*' Marley's Ghost wasn't only talking about Scrooge's nearest and dearest, and this would have been true even if Scrooge had actually had a real family.

And so this book, *The Customer-Centric You* must inevitably be about the need to *care about strangers.*

When we focus on this point, we do start to realise just how much *How To Win Friends and Influence People, A Christmas Carol* and *It's a Wonderful Life* have in common. The truth is that these three works are all, at one level, virtually text books on the craft – or perhaps one should say, the art – of caring about strangers.

Thumb back, for example, to the section and precepts of *How To Win Friends and Influence People*. Surely it's self-evident that central to all the sections and precepts there is the one guiding rule: *care genuinely about the agenda of others*.

The fact is, if most human beings weren't so selfish the world wouldn't need such books.

If most human beings weren't so selfish, the world wouldn't need Jesus Christ to tell us to love our neighbours as ourselves.

If human beings weren't so selfish, the world wouldn't need Dale Carnegie to tell us that, at heart, the way to win friends and influence people is to care *genuinely* about the strangers who you would like to win as friends and who you would like to influence. The world wouldn't need Charles Dickens to tell us that any creed or 'philosophy' that places the cold needs of organisational life and technology above the needs of the individual human heart is bound to lead to social disaster and is also doomed to implode.

Nor would the world need Dickens to point out to us, in the story of Ebeneezer Scrooge, that when we *do* lose interest in the agenda and happiness of strangers – that is, our fellow human beings on this extremely small planet that is careering through space many light-years from any other world that might have some form of life on it – it is ultimately *we* who suffer, because we lose contact with a vital part of ourselves.

Great religious leaders tend to preach along these lines, too. In most religions, and certainly in Christianity, the religious concept of 'heaven', or in whatever terms the religion describes it, can be interpreted not only as some utopia where we will enjoy everlasting happiness after our death but also as a blissful state of being we can achieve *here on Earth when we live infused with a true and genuine love of our fellow creatures.*

In *A Christmas Carol*, a passage of great relevance here occurs near the end of the story, the passage where Scrooge realises that it *is* still Christmas morning, and that he can now atone for his years of his appalling act of permitting the better side of his nature to shrivel into a frigid, grey, half-dead wizened thing that is entirely indifferent to the agenda of strangers (or even what remains of his family). Scrooge realises that he can resuscitate his own spirit, and become the person he is capable of being, and in doing so he understands and it's a great shock — that the first beneficiary of his new-found generosity of spirit towards other human beings is, in fact, *himself.*

> *He went to church, and walked about the streets, and watched the people hurrying to and fro, and patted children on the head, and questioned beggars, and looked down into the kitchens of houses, and up to the windows; and found that everything yield him pleasure. He had never dreamed that any walk — that anything — could give him so much happiness.*

Ultimately, the entire Christian religious message may, at heart, boil down to urging us to care deeply and sincerely about others. This, at least, appears to be the view of David Lodge, the popular and immensely talented British novelist. His novel *Paradise News* (1991) takes a witty look at sex and religion while managing to be inspirational about them both. The novel concerns — among other things — Bernard, an academic Catholic theologian with doubts who goes to Hawaii to comfort a dying relative and finds true love there for the first time in his life. Lodge was himself brought up as a Catholic and has called himself an 'agnostic Catholic'.

There is a remarkable passage near the end of the book (this particular passage does not contain any plot spoilers, by the way) which, in the guise of a lecture being given by Bernard, sets down what might perhaps be described as a reverential secular take on religion, in the form of a lecture he is giving his students.

In our terms here in *The Customer-Centric You,* this powerful and intriguing passage in effect links a summary of the nature of the customer-centricity — that it involves caring sincerely about the agenda of strangers — with the core of the Christian message.

'There is a passage in Matthew, Chapter 25, which seems particularly relevant here. Matthew is the most explicitly apocalyptic of the synoptic gospels, and this section of it is sometimes referred to by scholars as the Sermon on the End. It concludes with the well-known description of the Second Coming and the Last Judgement:

> **When the Son of Man comes in his glory, escorted by all the angels, then he will take his seat on the throne of glory. All the nations will be assembled before him and he will separate men one from another as the shepherd separates sheep from goats. He will place the sheep on his right hand and the goats on his left.**

Pure myth. But on what grounds does Christ the King separate the sheep from the goats? Not, as you might expect, fervency of religious faith, or orthodoxy of religious doctrine, or regularity of worship, or observance of the Commandments, or indeed anything 'religious' at all.

> **Then the King will say to those on his right hand, 'Come, you whom my Father has blessed, take for your heritage the kingdom prepared for you since the foundation of the world. For I was hungry and you gave me food; I was thirsty and you gave me drink; I was a stranger and you made me welcome; naked and you clothed me, sick and you visited me, in prison and you came to see me.' Then the virtuous will say to him in reply, 'Lord when did we see you hungry and feed you; or thirsty and give you drink?' When did we see you a stranger and make you welcome; naked and clothe you; sick or in prison and go to see you?' And the King will answer, 'I tell you solemnly, insofar as you did this to the least of these brothers of mine, you did it to me.'**

The virtuous seem quite surprised to be saved, or to be saved for **this** reason, doing good in an unselfish but pragmatic and essentially this-worldly sort of way. It's as if Jesus left this essentially humanist message knowing that one day all the *supernatural mythology in which it was wrapped would have to be discarded.'*

I honestly don't think it matters very much whether this is what Lodge himself feels (though I think it very possible he does) or whether Lodge is only presenting these thoughts as something that Bernard is thinking at this stage in the story. The real point here is that the novel is suggesting, in a truly moving way, that the Christian message, even if stripped of all its (as agnostics would say) mythology, remains a mighty, vital and life-enhancing message.

I believe this is also true of the customer-centricity mindset, which I would summarise here as *the state of mind in which you not only are willing to care sincerely about the agenda of strangers, but actively enjoy doing so.*

I believe that really caring about the agenda of others very soon makes *your* life more fulfilling, more emotional, more satisfying, more illuminating and more charged with inspiration and meaning.

Why? Because when you really do care about the agenda of others, you are – by definition – infinitely more part of the life of the world than when you only live dingily to pursue your own agenda.

Adopting the customer-centricity mindset makes life wondrous, inspiring, illuminating, and ultimately great fun. You will be at one with all of humanity, not only with your friends and family.

The first benefit of a truly customer-centric mindset really will be YOU.

What next?

So far, in Part One of this book, I've explored customer-centricity from a wide range of perspective and viewpoints.

Now, in Part Two, through a combination of guidance, suggestions and case studies, I look at how making customer-centricity happen in practical situations.

PART TWO

MAKING CUSTOMER-CENTRICITY HAPPEN

6

AN ACTION PLAN TO BRING CUSTOMER-CENTRICITY INTO ANY ORGANISATION

Initial thoughts

This chapter is about how customer-centricity can be implemented at a practical level in any organisation.

The first thing to say is that an organisation can only become more customer-centric if it wants to become so. In the same way that no-one who is ill is likely to be susceptible to being cured, even by the best of doctors, if that person does not *wish* to get cured, an organisation can only be infused with customer-centricity if that's what the organisation wants.

This said, it's unlikely that every person at an organisation will wish for the infusion. Many people will be perfectly happy with the status quo, normally because that status quo gives them safe niches in which they are not unduly troubled by arduous labour or effort.

However, you'll have read enough of *The Customer-Centric You* to know that such a status quo is no more worth preserving than was Scrooge's state of mind at the start of *A Christmas Carol*.

In practice what usually happens is that senior management at an organisation decide to want to infuse the organisation with customer-centricity and everyone else at the organisation needs to follow suit if they want to keep their jobs.

But picking up on the point that being compelled to become more customer-centric is nowhere near as good as having a natural desire for this, it really does help if other people at the organisation beyond senior management really wish to improve the organisation's focus on customers.

This is a vital point, as it is too easy for senior management to get interested in customer-centricity as a *theoretical* idea, whereas in practice customer-centricity, being such a practical strategy in itself, needs to be implemented in a correspondingly practical way. It's very often the case that it is the personnel further down the hierarchy who are most involved with actually *delivering* customer-centricity at a practical level.

I personally believe that change is the most important challenge organisations face. Customer-centricity is vital because it lets you cope with change.

Will technology do the job for us?

The point about technology in any application is that it is a fundamentally neutral dynamic: neither inherently good or bad, but its effectiveness depends purely on what the application is. Essentially, technology is simply an enormously powerful tool and unquestionably if the tool is applied in the right way, it can help us achieve objectives that were very likely unimaginable before.

In any practical application within an organisation, *technology* will only be effective if the job it is required to do is the right job. Because technology is indeed only a tool, it will only be effective if first of all the organisation's attitude and approach has been got right.

When it comes to implementing customer-centricity in an organisation, technology will only be effective if the organisation has first properly restructured itself and reorganised itself at a practical, conceptual and customer-focused level.

If the restructuring and re-engineering of the organisation has first taken place, the use of the right kind of technology to advance customer-centricity may be very effective indeed. But imagining that technology can do the job unaided by that restructuring is a mistake.

It's like this: if someone is ill but would like to enjoy a day in town meeting their friends and doing some shopping, merely dragging them out of bed and forcing them to put some smart clothes on over their pyjamas, and then dragging them into town and round the shops is hardly likely to make for a happy experience. Instead, what needs to happen is that the patient must first be made well again, and then the patient can put on the clothes by himself or herself and enjoy a great day in town.

Technology implemented before a necessary restructuring and re-engineering has taken place is like the clothes put on that ill patient when the patient is still ill. The clothes may give a semblance of wellness, but the underlying illness will still be a problem.

What customer-centricity means in the relationship between an organisation and its customers

When an organisation has identified that it needs to infuse itself with customer-centricity, it will realise that, organisationally, it needs to make a journey from where it is now as far as customer-centricity is concerned, to where it wants to be.

How difficult the journey is will depend on how customer-centric the organisation is at present. But what will be clear is the need for the journey. This means that any practical activity directed around maximises an organisation's customer-centricity must inevitably start with an assessment of how customer-centric the organisation is at present.

The initial assessment

The initial assessment is founded on investigating the current organisational situation in relation to five crucial questions. These questions are as follows. Because the entire investigation and process here means looking at what the organisation does from the customer's agenda, the questions are deliberately designed to be asked by the customers:

1. **Is your organisation making it easy for me to deal with you?**
    This question relates to with the *process and organisation element* of the investigation.

2. **Does your organisation give me an enjoyable experience when I deal with you?**
   This question relates to the *customer engagement element* of the investigation.

3. **Does your organisation understand me?**
   This question relates to the *customer information process.*

4. **Does your organisation continually improve my experience as a customer?**
   This question relates to the *metrics element* of the investigation.

5. **Does your organisation present me with products and services that delight me?**
   This question relates to the *product development element* of the investigation.

If the answer to all these questions is an emphatic yes, the organisation is likely already to be infused with an abundance of customer-centricity. But in practice few organisations are likely to be in the privileged position of having the answers to all these questions being an emphatic affirmative.

What's more likely is that the affirmatives will be much less emphatic and/or that some questions could only be answered in the negative.

The process of investigating answers to these questions may involve specialised assistance or at the very least will require an organisation to take a dispassionate and vigorous look at itself in the light of these questions. The reason for sometimes using an external specialist to help with the investigation or indeed to carry it out is that some matters may be raised during the investigation which the organisation would rather not talk about. Even the most customer-centric members of staff may have areas in their daily work where they are not particularly customer-centric.

Another problem is that while no-one is ever likely to be *explicitly* opposed to customer-centricity, what matters is their behaviour towards customers or in relation to activities that form part of a customer experience.

As we've seen, the product development element of an organisation can be especially inflexible and change-resistant, simply because re-designing products in a radical sense and rethinking what exactly the organisation is supplying to its customers is an extremely demanding process and the people involved with the status quo in product development are especially likely to be concerned about their jobs if radical change were to come.

But sometimes radical change is the only answer.

A specialised outside organisation that is carrying out the investigation – or perhaps some sort of 'action squad' within the organisation – will need to run exercises, workshops and customer surveys that provide answers to the above five questions. During this process of investigation, the following strategic dynamics also need to be investigated:

- the overall level of customer-centricity within the organisation
- the level of understanding of what customer-centricity actually is in the organisation's terms
- a clear perception of the scope the organisation has to become more focused around its customers
- the time frames involved for attaining maximum customer-centricity
- the costs involved for attaining maximum customer-centricity
- all the constraints on customer-centricity that must be eliminated
- a comprehensive understanding of all the different customers the organisation has and what precisely they want from the organisation.

To recap: this last question is of maximum importance because it will help to define where the organisation should be going in the future. Knowing what customers want from the organisation is, as we've seen, much more than just knowing what *products* the organisation wants. Remember the typewriter manufacturers who never made the successful transition to word-processors. Their mistake, as we've seen, was that they saw themselves as providing typewriters whereas in fact what they were providing was the ability for customers to create and process documents. And this leads to a crucial general point:

> *Don't be misled into thinking that what your customers want from you is necessarily the product or service you are selling. What they really want from you may very well be something more general: a need that the product or service only meets in a limited way at present.*

Of course, customers very likely will not even know what they really want until it is made available to them. Technological development creates new products that customers did not know even existed until they became available, but *that isn't an excuse for organisations to be ignorant of what their customers really want from them.*

It seems to me that a powerful example here is how the way in which we spend our evenings has changed dramatically over, say, the past century.

Of course, some of the things that people did one hundred years ago are the same as now, but many of the activities are different. A century ago television had not been invented beyond a few initial ideas, and while radio existed, it was not yet a mass-market consumer product. When people were indoors, they spent their evenings playing cards or games, or playing music on the family piano or harmonium if they had one, or in other kinds of pursuits such as keeping scrap-books and so on. All the organisations which have provided products or services to meet those needs, have not *really* been supplying the products and services so much as meeting the needs for people to pass their leisure time in an interesting way.

The need for people to pass their leisure time in an interesting way has not changed; what has changed is the nature of the products they have used in order to do that.

A hundred years ago, for example, a major consumer product

was sheet music which you could buy and then use to play music at home on whatever instruments you had. It is difficult now, when music is available electronically and from so many different sources, to imagine a time when the only way people could enjoy music was by playing it themselves on musical instruments or by going to concerts. The poet Samuel Taylor Coleridge's famous reference to church bells as the 'poor man's only music' only really acquires its true poignancy when you reflect there was a time when this was indeed the case.

The reason why sheet music is no longer a mass consumer product is ultimately because most people prefer the more passive activity of watching television or listening to the radio to playing their own music.

If the organisations that supplied sheet music to customers (and a hundred years ago it was quite routine for famous pieces of music to sell more than one million copies in sheet form) had been more in tune (if you'll forgive the pun) with their customers' real needs, these organisations themselves would have been first off the post when, in the 1920s, television began to be an achievable technology. After all, the sheet-music organisations had the capital to invest in new technology such as television, or indeed radio. However, while sheet-music organisations did in some cases get involved in the expansion of technologies such as the phonograph (the ancestor of the record-player) they did not get involved in other kinds of leisure technology.

Even in our own lifetimes we have seen the extraordinary proliferation of computer-based entertainment and the development of digital television supplied by a computer. It is already the case that more people watch TV via their computer than via a standard television.

Without elaborating on this point any more, we again see the vital need for an organisation to have a real perception of what it is truly offering its customers. *For most organisations, the first step they take towards achieving true customer-centricity happens when they really start to delve into gaining an understanding of what their customers really want from them.*

The 'stick of rock' effect

The overall objective for which an organisation should aim is a re-structuring of the organisation that results in every person actively involved with the organisation in any way doing everything they can to further customer-centricity within the organisation.

Here's a useful way of illustrating the overall effect for which the organisation should be striving.

In the past, and still in many cases today, an integral part of the British experience of visiting the seaside was the purchase of a stick of a hard cylindrical stick of a confection known (not unreasonably) as 'rock'. Rock is typically flavoured with mint and is genuinely dangerous for one's dental resources if one bites into it too hard. However, when you do bite into it you realise the interesting fact that sticks of rock are made with the same motif (typically happy phrases such as 'Welcome to Brighton') *running all the way through the stick.*

This has always seemed to me a most ingenious technical achievement. I still don't know how it's done. But the point is that the stick of rock manages to pursue its welcoming customer-friendly message throughout its entire structure.

Indeed, a stick of rock is about as customer-centric a thing as it's possible to imagine. It delivers its welcome, its sweetness, its flavour throughout its entire being, and for many people biting into it and wondering if your teeth will survive the experience is all part of the fun.

The message that runs through the entire stick of rock is exactly like the role customer-centricity should play within an organisation. Every part of the organisations should be infused with the same belief in customer-centricity that is being put into practice in everything the organisation does.

Organisations should use their human, capital, know-how, operational and technological resources to create the 'stick of rock' effect throughout their entire organisation, with the effect being not to deliver the stick of rock's message but rather comprehensive customer-centricity.

The high-level relationship diagram

The next step in the process to make the organisation fully customer-centric will depend to some extent on who is doing the engineering.

At Charteris, the consultancy with which I am involved, we create a blueprint for customer-centricity that we refer to as the 'high-level relationship diagram'.

This diagram sets out the current relationship that exists between the organisation, its various departments, its external partners, its products and services and its customers.

The diagram is designed to allow these current relationships to be fully understood and plotted in order that they can be where necessary enhanced, or where also necessary dismantled in order to bring customer-centricity to the entire organisation.

The illustration below, of just one example of a high-level relationship diagram, shows how the relationships are 'mapped' and linked to one another as part of the process of maximising an organisation's customer-centricity.

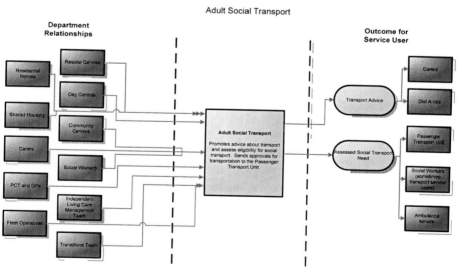

Adult Social Transport

Notes:
Use of local community centres rather than larger centralised day centres has increased the need for social transport. Transport reviews are not currently part of clients annual review process. Liaise with social care managers when service user needs change, affecting transport needs. Arrange and cancel transport. Referrals for transport go to team managers, or if extra costs are required, to a principal officer. WBC fleet operatives are very good at phoning social workers if there are any concerns with transport users.

Once the high-level relationship diagram has been finalised after the preparation of preliminary versions that are often modified following discussions with the client and following further research, the high-level relationship diagram becomes an extremely powerful tool that acts as a catalyst for the entire process of making an organisation fully customer-centric.

Here now is a tried and tested eight-point plan for maximising customer-centricity within your organisation:

1. Identify who your primary and secondary customers are.
2. Identify the products and services they consume and through which channels (web, call centre, bricks and mortar and so on).
3. Work out where the crucial 'points of addition' occur in adding value to those products and services.
4. Make sure each of the business areas involved in these points of addition *know* how they — the business areas — add value to these products and services.
5. Align the organisational structure to support these points of addition.
6. Minimise the activities that don't add value to what the customer is getting from the organisation.
7. Ensure that the correct measurements maintain and improve the processes.
8. Support all the above, where appropriate, with technology solutions.

7

EXTRA SALES *AND* REDUCED COSTS – THE KILLER APPLICATIONS OF CUSTOMER-CENTRICITY

Initial thoughts

All new technologies have 'killer applications': that is those particularly potent applications that most abundantly justify the technology. For example, the killer application of the cathode-ray tube is the television and other screen-based displays.

I don't know why the phrase 'killer applications' has come into general usage; very likely it's to do with the unfortunate fact that, generally speaking, the moment human beings develop a technology, they look to see if there is any application of it that will involve destroying fellow human beings. I suppose this applies to nuclear fission, for example, in a way that I do not need to spell out.

Strategic concepts also have killer applications. In the case of customer-centricity, there are two killer applications. These are:

- selling
- cost reduction

The great thing about these two killer 'apps' is that, *if customer-centricity is properly applied within an organisation, the organisation can enjoy the benefits of extra sales and cost reductions.*

On the face of it improving sales performance and reducing costs are mutually exclusive goals. One would imagine that increasing sales requires resources to be devoted to this objective, and those resources are bound to cost money.

But the truth is different. The truth, which I personally regard as one of the most exciting aspects of customer-centricity, is that *the very process of implementing customer-centricity creates a streamlining within an organisation that should ideally introduce the highest levels of customer focus into all the processes and activities of the organisation, which, if properly engineered, should indeed yield increased sales at reduced costs.*

Why? Because the extra customer focus will mean that customers' needs are being met more thoroughly and more extensively by the organisation, and the fact that this is so will reduce costs because of the fundamental streamlining of the organisation that has resulted from the enhanced customer-centricity.

And so customer-centricity is truly thrilling for an organisation, because if properly applied, it can meet the organisation's two primary objectives: extra revenue from extra sales and lower costs.

That is the benefit in private sector terms. In the public sector, the extra sales correspond to extra levels of service being delivered. Cost reductions, however, in the public sector are no less important than in the private sector. Indeed, they may be more important because in the public sector the money being spent is the taxpayer's money.

At a logical level, the discipline of infusing an organisation with customer-centricity teaches us to focus on everything that adds value to the customer. By doing this, we reduce – or eliminate – the amount of time being devoted to activities and processes within the organisation that *don't* add value to the customer. We are back with the concept of the need for an organisation to devote at least 70 percent of its effort to things that add value to the customer.

The cost reductions arise because once an organisation has been comprehensively 'audited' from a customer-centricity perspective, anything that doesn't add value to the customer will have been scrutinised and if necessary eliminated.

There is a famous business story that in the days when matches were more of a major consumer product than they are today, a match company that made match boxes with a striking surface on two of the box's sides was advised by a customer that it was perfectly sufficient to have only one striking surface. This is a good example of customer-centricity at work.

Indeed, quite often, organisations become ingrained with doing superfluous things, frequently because there is a tradition within the organisation that it was okay to do this. It may even be the case that people at the organisation have actually forgotten why a particularly unnecessary process or activity was introduced in the first place, but like a winding path through a field, the origins of the winding nature of it may indeed have been forgotten.

What is certain is that most, if not all, organisations, no matter how much they may like to regard themselves as efficient, will on careful analysis be revealed to incubate and often enshrine unnecessarily complex processes that either add no value to the customer or add insufficient value to justify the existence of the process.

It's the same with government spending: this is also often based around processes and activities that are felt to be necessary but which often aren't. By increasing the level of customer-centricity in the process, the efficiency of the process can be dramatically increased, and costs reduced.

So now here is Hewett's Second Law:

Customer-centricity is the holy grail of all professional activities because, properly implemented, it can lead to the winning of additional revenue as well as cost reductions.

Now let's look at selling and cost reduction separately.

Selling

Selling is a killer app for customer-centricity because every organisation has to sell, and customer-centricity will let you do it better.

Quite apart from the sheer enormous benefits that customer-centricity offers to the discipline of selling, there is a vital subsidiary benefit of customer-centricity within the selling arena. This is that, properly used, the *information gathered at the point of sale* can play a tremendous role in defining what is likely to be of vital importance to the customer in the future.

After all, one of my central philosophies, as discussed in the previous chapter, is that people do not so much buy what precisely meets their needs, as what they regard as the best approximation to meeting their needs from what is available in the marketplace.

This must be the case, otherwise there would be no market for earlier iterations of products that have improved with technological and practical progress.

It follows that anyone who is genuinely and deeply committed to customer-centricity should not only be interested in making the sale, but in finding out during the process of making the sale as much about customer needs as is feasible.

Of course, many organisations do this, with varying degrees of success, though in the majority of organisations, the culture of 'closing' the sale is far more dominant than the culture of finding out exactly what the customer wants.

Indeed, in the financial services sector, there's long been an unfortunate tradition of the sale meaning far more to the organisation than finding out about customer requirements. The very word 'close' when used to describe the completion of a sale, seems to symbolise that once the sale is completed, the organisation feels that there is a sense in which the customer has reached the end of its need to take real trouble to woo the customer. Thinking like this is like thinking that a successful honeymoon means that neither of the two people who are married need to make any more effort to make the marriage work.

If nothing else, the intense competition faced in most industry sectors in current challenging economic times, means that organisations in most sectors are having the sense to stop thinking like this. The truth is that the sale should be the start of the relationship with the customer much as a honeymoon should be the start of a marriage. After all, if – and I believe it is incontestable that this is the case – the customer is essentially buying the best approximation of what they want rather than what they would ideally want, it means that the customer must, by definition, be open to the possibility of buying something better from someone else.

One of the reasons why market research is such an exciting profession to work in is that the profession is really at the knife-edge of what customers really want, and can offer exciting insights into customer attitudes and what prompts specific buying decisions. This is one reason why I included so much of Professor David Thomson's thinking earlier in the book about sensory signatures.

Needs and wants and their relationship to Customer-centricity and selling

Customers buy things because they either feel that they *need* the things or *want* the things. We have already looked at the difference between the concepts of customer needs and customer wants, and looked at how these concepts acquire a particular importance in situations – such as when services are being delivered by a local authority, where the organisation delivering the services is likely to be limited in the resources to which it has access.

In the case of local authorities, the reason why the resources are limited is because in many cases the resources are not being paid for directly by the customer, and there will always be more demand for such services than the supply available. Where the resources are not limited, such as in any situation where an organisation is selling products or services to customers on a purely commercial basis, the distinction between customer needs and customer wants remains of great importance, especially for any organisation that truly seeks to deliver customer-centricity.

The point is that an organisation that is only delivering customer *wants* may soon find that customers start to distrust it if the organisation does not take some care to ascertain whether the wants are genuine ones. If the wants are born from limited information, which as we have seen is often the case, customers may appreciate being guided to what they really *need* rather than to what they conceive that they want.

Indeed, in some cases, there is even statutory legislation to prevent organisations from selling what customers do not really need, especially where the product or service is complex and customers might reasonably complain that they could not possibly have had the information required in order to buy what they actually *need*.

An obvious example of an industry to which this applies is the financial industry, where financial service organisation selling certain types of product such as insurance and pension plans are under a statutory duty to ascertain the precise nature of the need for the particular product on the part of the customer. Where the product has been sold in essential contravention to what the customer really needs, there is ample opportunity for the customer to take legal action against the seller and in many cases organisations employing sellers who have not done their job properly face substantially fines as well as publicity that has jeopardised their overall activities.

In other cases, such as – to go back to the example of luxury watches or other luxury items such as expensive cars – the seller needs to factor into the thinking that the customer's needs are not only going to be a result of the customer's practical requirements (after all, any kind of watch will tell you the time and any kind of reliable car will get you from A to B), but also the emotional satisfaction that the customer gains from the product is an issue in ascertaining what the customer's needs are.

Ultimately, it is unquestionable in delivering true customer-centricity, an organisation must truly understand customer needs – as well as wants. It is very likely that, sooner or later, any customer whose wants are being met by a supplier who is less interested in meeting the customer's needs, is going to start resenting the seller and will feel – possibly with justification – that the seller is more interested in making the sale than in understanding what the customer really needs.

A highly entertaining movie that depicts salesmen (and they are all men in this particular case) selling customers what they don't need (or – in many cases, don't actually want) is the movie *Boiler Room* (2000), which is also remarkable for a wonderful and often hilarious monologue acted by movie star Ben Affleck on the fun of earning large amounts of money.

On a more serious note, I believe that selling successfully over any sustained period is only possible if you really know what your customers need, and for this reason we now move on to what factors motivate a purchase.

The factors that lead to a purchase being made

Generally, in order for a particular purchase to be made, the following factors need to be in place from a customer's point of view:

- the customer likes what is on offer and feels that buying it would improve his or her life at least sufficiently to justify the price
- the customer can afford the purchase (or, is happy to open a credit line to facilitate the purchase)
- the customer must feel that the timing is right
- the customer must gain some sort of psychological gratification from the purchase

This last point here even applies to purchases – such as, say, an insurance policy – that offer no real benefit except peace of mind. This benefit, however, is – as we have seen – exactly what the insurance *does* confer. All purchases do need to give customers a psychological benefit, and the greater the understanding an organisation has of the psychological benefits their products and services confer, the greater the likelihood that the organisation will be truly customer-centric.

The need for an organisation to have a deep understanding of its customers in order to sell effectively

Most organisations claim that they know their customers well, but in most cases this claim is about as sincere as when chief executives address industry conferences on a Friday afternoon to proclaim that 'our people are our most important asset' and then begin a round of lay-offs on Monday morning.

The usual problem is this: most organisations are really only interested in their customers insofar as it allows them to make a quick sale.

It's not always entirely the organisations' fault. After all, they're competing in difficult markets themselves, and they need to keep the cost of the sale down. It's all very well for customers to complain that organisations are not particularly interested in them, but if the price of goods and services went up as a result of organisations spending longer on sales and taking longer to get to know customers, customers would soon complain.

All the same, the cost issue, which is of course something we've already looked at, is not a viable excuse for failing to have a deep understanding of customers.

The deeper your understanding of customers, the more knowledge you have of them and what they need, the easier the sale is because the more customer-centric you will be.

Too many organisations assume from the start that finding customers will be difficult and take for granted that they must spend a lot of time and money on approaching customers even though they know that most will not want to buy. If more of this time and money was spent on gaining a deeper understanding of the marketplace and the customers who inhabit it, it would be much easier to sell and there would not be so much wastage in the process of going to market and trying to find customers.

Indeed, organisations should start trying to cultivate a deeper understanding of customers by first looking after their existing customers properly and giving *them* everything the customer needs. It is almost always the case that winning new business from an existing customer is easier than winning it cold from a completely new customer.

As to what this deeper understanding of customers consists of, that will vary from customer to customer. But ultimately, customers buy in order to gain a psychological gratification, and so the more you know about their own psychology the better, not because you want to *take advantage* of this psychology, but simply because you want to know what makes your customers really tick, what makes them happy, what they regard as timely, what their life goals are, and what they can afford.

Mark McCormack, in *What They Don't Teach You at Harvard Business School*, has an excellent anecdote, which goes a long way towards explaining what really understanding a customer's psychology really means. As Mark McCormack says:

*I was amused recently by an article in the **New York Times** on Morgan Stanley & Company, the aristocratic investment banking firm which hires only the top MBAs. Morgan Stanley had beaten out twelve other firms in vying for the right to manage the Teamsters Union's $4.7 billion pension fund. Here's what the **Times** had to say:*

'At one of their meetings with a committee of Teamsters trustees – union men and trucking executives – part of the session was devoted to the Morgan officers' individual backgrounds, with the emphasis on humble origins.

'One executive said that a scholarship put him through college. Another pointed out that he had joined the Marine Corps directly after school. And a third told the trustees sitting across the table that he had grown up in a modest household, the son of a railroad engineer. So it went as each of a dozen or more Morgan officials took his turn.

'It was as if they said, "I know we have this portrait of J.P. Morgan up on the wall, but we're really regular guys," said one participant, who asked not to be named.'

Anyone who can convince the Teamsters that J.P. Morgan was, at heart, a union man, understands the importance of selling.

I would agree with Mark McCormack that this anecdote shows an impressive understanding of the importance of selling. But I would say that it actually shows something else, possibly even more: namely the importance of caring enough about customers to bother understanding them properly and caring about their agenda.

Anyone who really takes the trouble to find out what their customers need, and who also cares about their agenda, should find that, within reason, getting sales will be comparatively easy.

I'm not suggesting that selling things is *ever* totally easy. I think there's always going to be some wastage when prospecting, by which I mean time and effort spent identifying and approaching prospects who may become customers. In practice, there is always going to be a limit on what we know about what people want until we know them well, and we can't usually know them well until they actually become customers, so the whole business of prospecting is inevitably something of a double-edged sword. That said, I think too many organisations take for granted that they will need to spend a lot of time on prospecting when, instead, they would do better to focus on a small number of prospects and really try to find out what the agenda of these prospects is.

After all, the internet offers innumerable opportunities to find out about people and organisations before one approaches them. If you don't take the trouble to do your internet research, at the very minimum, do you deserve to have the customer in the first place?

Cost reduction

Extensive experience in implementing customer-centricity programmes within the private and public sectors, has taught me that the way to achieve maximum cost reductions is not so much to be obsessive about trying to *achieve* cost reductions but, rather, *to be obsessive about making customers the focus of everything you do.*

Carrying out this prime directive will, in most cases, *automatically* engender cost reductions because the dead wood and flabby processes that have incurred high costs will be eliminated completely.

You'll remember what Gordon Gekko thought about the highly-paid executives at Teldar Paper in his famous speech in the movie *Wall Street*. He certainly thought of *them* as mostly dead wood or – one might say – waste paper.

As far as the practicalities of putting a total spotlight on customers that will lead to cost reductions is concerned, the next two chapters – which, respectively, show customer-centricity in action in real life cases in the private sector and then in the public sector – give plenty of examples of how it works. In particular, the case study that features in Chapter 9 about Wiltshire Council in the UK offers comprehensive practical information about how to maximise customer-centricity in the public sector and as a result win extensive cost reductions.

8

CUSTOMER-CENTRICITY IN ACTION IN THE PRIVATE SECTOR

These four case studies all illuminate the application of customer-centricity in the private sector. The case studies I look at here cover a wide range of activities, but all have in common the great energy, resourcefulness and dedication that has been applied to focusing on customers.

The four case studies are:

1. **The 'Dabbawallahs' of Mumbai** – a remarkable example of customer-centricity in a highly successful private food delivery system in India's most densely populated city

2. **The Tesco Clubcard** – the most successful customer loyalty card in Britain

3. **The John Lewis Partnership** – a major UK retail chain renowned for its attention to customers

4. **Majestic Wine** – a leading wine retailer that has achieved enormously rapid growth through a complete, sincere focus on customer-centricity achieved substantially through a particular approach to recruiting, training and managing staff.

The 'Dabbawallahs' of Mumbai – lunches delivered with real customer-centricity

If you love Indian food, you'll very likely enjoy this case study, which along with Charles Dickens's account of the shops Scrooge sees on Christmas morning, is the only part of *The Customer-Centric You* that you could almost eat.

As you'll know if you *do* love Indian food, what makes an Indian meal delicious is the variety of what's on offer, spicy curried meats, exquisite vegetables such as lentils and other pulses, cauliflower, okra, fresh onions, all made to deliver a tremendous taste treat that is, to use the term introduced earlier in this book by the consumer psychologist Professor David Thomson, a 'spike of positivity'. Admit it, aren't you hungry already?

Well, by midday the workers of Mumbai (formerly Bombay) in India certainly are. This isn't too surprising because quite apart from their hard work during the day, Mumbai – with more than 19,000 people on average per square kilometre, is Indian's most densely populated city, and the enormous congestion of Mumbai's traffic means that workers have to set off for work very early in order to get to work on time.

The problem, though, is that Mumbai workers tend to prefer their lunches to consist of a precise array of dishes cooked by their wives (all right, all right, it's the twenty-first century, so I'll say life partners). But because the workers have to leave home so early in the morning, often between 5.00 and 6.00 a.m., their wives would practically need to start cooking their lunches in the middle of the night if the workers were to be able to take it along to work with them.

There's a customer need if ever there was one.

Step forward the hard-working operatives of the Mumbai Tiffin Box Suppliers Association, a group of about 5,000 lunch delivery men who are known in Mumbai as *dabbawallahs*. The word *dabbawallah* is from the local Marathi language, with *dabba* meaning a box (in practice, in the case of the *dabbawallahs*, a cylindrical tin or aluminium container), while *wallah* – a word every British expatriate in India knew during the days of the Raj – is technically speaking a suffix meaning the doer of a particular action, though a more straightforward idiomatic translation would be 'chap' or 'bloke'. *Dabbawallahs* are the chaps who carry the boxes.

After their husbands have set off for work, their wi-- life partners start cooking their meal, making all the favourite dishes that the husband likes and packing it in a dabba with a variety of compartments. Then, in around the mid-morning, the dabba is collected, usually on bicycle, by a 'collecting dabbawallah'. Each dabba has some sort of distinguishing mark on it, such as a particular colour or symbol: this is important because many dabbawallahs can't read or write. The collecting dabbawallahs take all the boxes to a local sorting place, where the boxes are sorted and bundled into groups, depending on their destinations. The bundled dabbas are loaded onto trains, with other sets of markings used to identify the railway station where the boxes are to be unloaded and the actual building where the boxes are to be delivered. The process is to some extent made easier by many trains carrying a designed coach for the dabbas.

At the right station, the dabbas are unloaded and handed over to a 'local dabbawallah', who delivers them to their hungry recipients. By this time most of the food is only lukewarm, but the workers often prefer it this way. (As one can imagine, wives sometimes communicate with their husbands by putting little notes inside the dabbas, but with the rise of instant messaging techniques such as texting on mobile phones, the more manual form of communications appears to be reducing.)

The scale of the dabbawallahs' operation is prodigious. About 200,000 lunch boxes get moved every day by around 5,000 dabbawallahs. The service is growing, at about five percent a year. The fee for the service is small (about £7 or $US11 per month), indeed almost only nominal, which it has to be, for wages for most workers in Mumbai are not high.

Yet what is most remarkable about the service offered by the dabbawallahs is in its phenomenal reliability. One survey found that they make less than one mistake per six million deliveries.

The tradition for great reliability of the dabbawallah system even extends to the service continuing throughout the severe weather that afflicts Mumbai during the monsoon system. Also, the local dabbawallahs and the local populations know each other well, and the bonds of trust they form help make the service run smoothly.

The reason for the accuracy is at heart a matter of mindset. It's true that the ingenious system of markings used to identify dabbas and their destinations, coupled with the well-organised system for conveying dabbas by rail, plays a vital role in maximising the reliability of the service they offer, but what really makes the dabbawallahs' system so effective is the sheer pride that they take in their work and in being part of the team.

The dabbawallah system does not use documentation at all; it would not be much use anyway, as so many of the dabbawallahs are illiterate. Nor is there a multiple or elaborate system of management, but just three layers.

Because the service is so inexpensive, wages for dabbawallahs are not high; about four thousand rupees per month (about £50 or $US80). You can live on that in Mumbai, but it isn't a lot. Also, each dabbawallah who joins the service is required to contribute a minimum capital in the form of two bicycles, a wooden crate, the white cotton uniform of the fraternity, and the trademark Gandhi cap the dabbawallahs wear, also known as a 'topi'. There is, however, a profit share, with the return on the dabbawallahs' capital being ensured by monthly division of the earnings of each individual dabbawallah unit.

The feeling of shared ownership unquestionably helps with the motivation of the dabbawallahs, but all the same the earnings remain quite small. Without high wages, the most powerful motivating force among them is the sheer pride in their work and in the traditions of the service. This pride in their work and in wanting to give customers a great experience is a big and fundamental part of the dabbawallahs' mindset, which is a clear, remarkable and extensive example of the customer-centricity mindset in action. The schedules of the service are jealously protected by the dabbawallahs: when British heir to the throne Prince Charles visited the dabbawallahs, he had to fit in with their schedule, rather than vice versa. The prince was so impressed with them that he even invited some to his wedding to Camilla Parker Bowles.

The dabbawallahs of Mumbai have been awarded Six Sigma accreditation, the business management strategy, originally developed by Motorola in 1981, that seeks to improve the quality of process outputs by identifying and removing the causes of defects (errors) and minimising variability in manufacturing and business processes.

The dabbawallah service has also been awarded ISO9000 accreditation for quality assurance. Dabbawallahs have even been invited to speak about the service at some of India's leading business schools.

The dabbawallah service originated during the days of British rule in India, when British people working in what was then Bombay did not like the local food that could be bought at restaurants and eating-houses in the city, so a delivery system was set up to ensure that they could have lunches – often consisting of the British-type food with which they were familiar – delivered to them from their homes. Ironically, since India's independence, the system is now used to convey Indian food to Indian workers. As for the British palate, which has demonstrated much more flexibility in what it is willing to get used to than one might, in the early part of the twentieth century, have imagined possible, it now positively tends to adore Indian food. There are more than 10,000 Indian restaurants (including takeaway-only restaurants) in London alone.

Until recently, the dabbawallahs and technology did not tend to mix. 'Our computers are our heads and our Gandhi caps are the covers that protect them from the sun and rain,' as one dabbawallah once said. But nowadays the dabbawallahs have a website and it is possible to hire the dabbawallah service through this and also by means of text messaging.

At heart, though, the service offered remains a resolutely manual one, carried out by operatives who take a great pride in their work and positively delight in giving their customers a superb experience at a modest cost.

The dabbawallahs are rather like some of the Parisian hotel and restaurant workers George Orwell describes in his short, moving and highly entertaining memoir *Down and Out in Paris and London* (1933). Orwell writes of certain hotel workers he had heard of who, despite their lowly wages, took immense pride in being, to use the French word that described them, *débrouillard*. That is, they took an enormous pride in getting a job done for customers no matter how difficult the job might seem to be, no matter how greatly the odds were stacked up against them.

As Orwell writes in particular of the *plongeurs* (dishwashers) he encountered:

> *Débrouillard is what every **plongeur** wants to be called. A **débrouillard** is a man who, even when he is told to do the impossible, will **se débrouiller**, get it done somehow.*

That quality of getting the job done for customers because they *are* customers and we want to do the very best for them, is of course, as we've seen, a major part of the customer-centricity mindset. Being customer-centric isn't only about having the mindset in one's overall attitude and outlook, and in one's strategic planning, it's also about getting one's hands dirty, and one's forehead into a sweat, in order to deliver a great service to customers. The *dabbawallahs* of Mumbai, like the *débrouillard* hotel workers of Paris, are great apostles of customer-centricity.

Let's celebrate this insight with an Indian takeaway, shall we?

Tesco Clubcard – an engine of massive customer-centricity success

The UK food retailer Tesco is a global grocery and general merchandising retailer. Tesco is currently the third largest retailer in the world measured by revenues and the second largest measured by profits. It has stores in 14 countries across Asia, Europe, and North America and is the grocery market leader in the UK (where it has a market share of about thirty percent), Malaysia and Thailand.

Tesco was founded by a businessman called Jack Cohen, who began his working life as an apprentice tailor to his father but in

1917 joined the Royal Flying Corps where he served as a canvas maker. Upon his demobilisation in 1919 he established himself as a market stall holder in Hackney, in London's East End by purchasing surplus army stock with the money he was given when he was demobilised.

Cohen soon became the owner of a number of market stalls, and started a wholesale business too. In 1924, he created the Tesco brand name from the initials of a tea supplier, T. E. Stockwell, and the first two letters of his own surname. The first Tesco store was opened in 1929. By 1939, Cohen owned a hundred Tesco stores.

Originally a UK-focused retailer specialising in food and drink, Tesco has diversified both geographically and by product, into a wide variety of others areas including financial services.

The Tesco Clubcard is the most successful loyalty card scheme that there has ever been in Britain. Indeed, it is arguably the most successful loyalty card scheme in the world, and it is regarded within the retail industry globally as a model of how such a scheme should be designed and how it should work.

Tesco, one of the UK's leading food retailers, began looking into loyalty schemes back in 1993, by collecting data from customers and then sending them targeted offers. In 1994, the Tesco executive responsible for Tesco's trials of a loyalty card attended a conference where a marketing expert, Clive Humby, from a company called dunnhumby was speaking. Dunnhumby, which offered marketing services, had already signed clients such as Cable & Wireless and BMW. Tesco began working with dunnhumby and throughout 1994 dunnhumby spearheaded a project that involved working with Tesco to find out more about its customers. When dunnhumby finally presented its finding, the then-Chairman of Tesco, Lord Maclaurin, said:

> *'What scares me about this is that you know more about my customers after three months than I know after 30 years.'*

The Tesco Clubcard was launched in 1995. The idea at the heart of it was to reward shoppers with points that were periodically transformed into vouchers that were sent to customers and could then be used as cash in Tesco stores. While the use of the vouchers was thus limited in this way, it could be argued that the vouchers amount to cash as people's weekly spend on food shopping is in effect a compulsory rather than discretionary spend and so having vouchers they can use in Tesco shops means they have an equivalent amount of cash spare to use for other purposes.

At first, the core principle at the heart of the card was that of a customer being awarded one point, which was worth a penny, for every pound spent (with a minimum spend of £1 applying for qualification). However, there have been some changes to this, with double points sometimes applying and with extra points being awarded if a customer purchases certain items.

The Tesco Clubcard is considered to have played an important role since 1995 as Tesco's rise to supremacy as the UK's leading food retailer by sales volume. The card is believed to have played a particular part in Tesco dominating Sainsbury in this respect, which was traditionally its biggest competitor. Sainsbury launched its own loyalty card in June 1996.

Today, the Tesco Clubcard now has about 15 million members in the UK, or more than 25 percent of the population. This includes many people who not do their regular weekly food shopping at Tesco. The precise reasons why the scheme has been so successful are a matter of opinion, but the following factors – all intimately linked with customer-centricity – are likely to have been key to the scheme's success:

- The association with Tesco, the largest food retailer in the UK, offers high visibility and an abundance of physical locations where customers can find out about the scheme.
- As I mention above, the scheme from the beginning had a fundamentally very simple premise: that you get back 1p for every £1 you spend. From August 2009 the scheme has been offering 2p for every £1 spent, a new benefit that increased the number of members by more than 1 million in the year following August 2009.
- Collecting points is easily done at the point-of-sale by the customer presenting a keyfob or card to the cashier who then

swipes it through a barcode reader. The self-check-out tills offer a similar facility, and on-line purchases load Clubcard points automatically if the customer is signed up.

- There are several other, essentially subsidiary, clubs associated with Clubcard. These include a wine club, a baby and toddler club, a healthy living club and a food club. The Clubcard scheme also offers a facility to save vouchers to be spent as Christmas approaches. This facility is rather like a Christmas savings scheme.

- Tesco has been adept at catching the mood of the time in the creativity it has applied to the Clubcard scheme. For example, the scheme now offers 'Green' Clubcard points awarded when customers either re-use bags when shopping in a store (one point is awarded per bag) or when customers opt out of receiving bagged products when shopping online (one point per ten unbagged items delivered).

- Tesco has also offered a limited-time scheme where customers can take their Clubcard points into stores and 'double them up' for goods within a number of departments.

- Tesco has recently launched a scheme whereby points may be collected by the customer on an iPhone, BlackBerry or Nokia Ovi by the customer presenting a barcode on the handset instead of a keyfob or card. This application is likely in the future to offer more functionality, including points balances and special offers.

- Overall, the Clubcard scheme allows Tesco to monitor particular buying preferences of individual customers through the swiping of their cards when they make their purchases. Quite apart from giving Tesco detailed insights that are useful for stocking and merchandising, this also allows individual customers to be targeted with offers. For example, when the Clubcard points spending vouchers are distributed by Tesco, they come accompanied with additional vouchers that offer additional Clubcard points to make additional particular purchases that Tesco has been able to see that the customer likes to make.

Obviously, the key factors about the Clubcard scheme are exclusive to Tesco, but the underlying ideas behind the scheme are, at least at one level, common sense. The lessons the success of the Clubcard scheme teaches us from a customer-centric point of view are, I think, as follows:

- All kinds of organisations with a large customer base of consumers, must commit to forging partnerships with third-parties who can help the organisation to enhance the customer proposition. At a very fundamental level Tesco did this when they began working with dunnhumby. More recently, Tesco forged all kinds of links with third parties in order to have new and different kinds of propositions to offer members of its Clubcard scheme. Creativity is required here too, to devise offerings customers are going to like, and this needs a deep understanding of customers: precisely the kind of understanding, in fact, that a loyalty scheme is likely to yield.

- Any organisation wishing to run a successful loyalty schemes need to have, or quickly develop, a genuine passion for understanding their customers. One factor in Tesco's success is that its customers tend to perceive it as sincere, genuinely concerned about them (even the Tesco slogan 'every little helps' implies an almost paternal concern) and very much plugged in to their lifestyle.

- Organisations need to build on their understanding of customers to create a real rapport with them.

- The premise at the heart of the loyalty scheme should be simple and powerful.

- Once the new affinity scheme is devised, it needs to be marketed and promoted with continuing passion and creativity.

- Customer databases must be used intelligently and creatively to assist with devising schemes and marketing them.

- Generally, there must be a genuinely good concept and branding. Time spent thinking hard about this and devising a great branding is never time wasted.

- There must be real self-belief in the run-up to launch and in the launch process itself.

A final point to make here is this. Customers always like to belong, and economic pressures will very likely increase customers' willingness to take part in a loyalty scheme that they feel will make their lives significantly better. Whatever the economic and social conditions, a really great loyalty scheme will always succeed, because no matter what pessimists may say, customers are always looking to have their lives enhanced.

The John Lewis Partnership – Value, Assortment, Service and Honesty

I admit, I have a personal reason for including the John Lewis Partnership (JLP) here: I spent fifteen years of my career as a partner – that is, employee with a share in the JLP's profits and I regard much of my thinking about customer-centricity to have been forged (a mixed metaphor, I admit, but I think appropriate in this case) on the shop-floors and in the offices of the JLP.

The JLP itself is unique among large UK retailers in that it is owned by its employees, who are all in effect its partners. JLP is a company that is owned by a trust on behalf of all its employees – its partners – who have a say in the running of the business and receive a share of annual profits, which is usually a significant addition to their salary. The nature of JLP means that it is a private company, unlike most organisations of a comparable size.

The JLP operates the John Lewis department stores, the Waitrose supermarkets and a company known as Greenbee which offers a range of financial services and other services via the internet. There is a JLP loyalty scheme which is attached to a JLP credit card and offers points that can be turned into vouchers. Note, however, that as the current rate of acceptance of credit card application across all sectors of the population is nowadays only about 20 percent, the JLP loyalty scheme cannot be regarded as a mass-market scheme like the Tesco Clubcard, and indeed the JLP loyalty scheme reflects the fact that JLP has traditionally targeted the wealthier sections of the population. More recently, however, the JLP has broadened its marketing strategy to embrace a wider range of buyers and has launched a lower-cost 'Value' range for the John Lewis shops and also the 'Essential' range for Waitrose. As well as this, Waitrose has been widely advertising that 1,000 of its most popular brands are no more expensive than at Tesco. All the same, Waitrose remains at heart a retail grocer for affluent people, selling a wide range of the highest-quality food and drink brands, many of which are not found in Tesco shops at all, or not in the smaller Tesco stores.

The business was founded in 1864 when John Lewis set up a draper's shop in Oxford Street, London, which developed into a department store. It was quite common for nineteenth-century specialised stores to diversity into department stores; for example, the world-famous department store Harrods of Knightsbridge was originally a grocery store in the 1830s (though its founder, Charles Henry Harrod, had started in business as a draper).

In 1905, John Lewis bought the Peter Jones store in Sloane Square. In 1920 his son, John Spedan Lewis, expanded earlier power-sharing policies by sharing the profits the business made among the employees. The democratic nature and profit-sharing basis of the business were developed into a formal partnership structure and Spedan Lewis bequeathed the company to his employees. There are currently about 70,000 partners – the majority full-time – working for the John Lewis Partnership.

The JLP's famous (though to many people slightly obscure) principle and slogan 'Never knowingly undersold' was adopted in 1925. It was created by Spedan Lewis and applied to the company's Peter Jones store. It stated that if a customer could buy the same item cheaper elsewhere they would refund the difference. Today, the company still honours this pledge, though the principle has been more refined, most notably to exclude online shopping.

In April 1933 the JLP bought Jessop & Son of Nottingham. This store was the first John Lewis outside London. The store kept the name 'Jessops' until 2002, when after a refurbishment and expansion the store was renamed as simply John Lewis. The partnership has also purchased a number of other regional department stores, as well as developing stores in new locations.

There are currently 31 John Lewis stores through the UK, 235 Waitrose supermarkets, as well as an on-line and catalogue business, and even a 4,000-acre John Lewis farm in Hertfordshire which is one of many suppliers of food and drink products to Waitrose.

For me, the JLP was where I really learned how into practice what has always been a passion to look after customers and offer them the level of service and quality of service that they wanted. I remember very vividly that from my very first week working there, I was struck with a powerful sense of how the JLP people I met came across to me as having a genuine, raw and instinctive knowledge of what customers wanted, along with a determination to meet those needs. By the time I joined the JLP, I'd worked in the aviation industry and already knew that I got a real kick out of finding out what my customers wanted and applying myself to their agenda, but at the JLP I was fortunate enough to be introduced at a formative time in my life (I was 21 years old when I joined the JLP for the first time) to a structure that really facilitated customer focus.

I attended the JLP training course in my first week, a course that everyone who joined the Partnership had to join. There, I was introduced to a four-word principle that stayed with me all the time I was at the Partnership and which has stayed with me ever since. This principle is VASH, which at the JLP stands for:

- **Value**
  Central to the JLP's entire thinking about customers is the need for them to be given what they perceive as value for money

- **Assortment**
  Also fundamental to JLP's own philosophy of customer-centricity is the need for customers to be offered a wide range of buying choices, which of course not only means a

wide assortment of products generally but also a wide range of options (such as in terms of size, colour and other variables) within a particular range.

- **Service**
  The quality of customer service at the JLP is something the Partnership prides itself on, in my view entirely justifiably. The attitude at JLP is that everything of significance that partners do at the JLP should be done with a view towards furthering the quality of customer service.

- **Honesty**
  Honesty here means honesty in how customers are treated. I remember that during the training course I attended as soon as I joined the JLP, a woman on the course asked the trainer what we should do if, for example, a lady customer comes to try on a dress, which the sales assistant thinks looks awful on her, but she – the customer – likes it. 'Should we conceal what we really feel,' the trainee asked, 'and tell her that the dress looks great on her?'

The trainer said emphatically that no, not telling the truth to customers was unacceptable. Instead, the sales assistant should suggest some other dresses which look better on her, and should if necessary point out why the dress does not perhaps suit her as well as she thought it did.

The JLP, in its philosophy of honesty, and indeed in its philosophy of VASH generally, is seeking in all it does to build long-term relationships with customers that are based around giving value, assortment, service and honesty to the customer throughout the entirety of the Partnership's relationship with the customer. This is the complete opposite of the 'hard sell' based around making a quick buck from customers, who will very likely soon realise that they have received neither value, assortment, service or honesty from the seller.

Many people talk about how fickle customers are during the internet age, when they can migrate to another seller merely by clicking on their mouse. That may indeed be, but few organisations selling across the internet – or in a physical sales environment – really do offer VASH. Yes, customers may be fickle, but the point is that they've always been fickle, they've always been ready to move on to another seller if they don't feel satisfied. Victorian housewives would have had no compunction at all about dropping a supplier of any of the medley of food and drink and household products they bought if they were not satisfied with the service offered. All that the internet age has done has been to make the process of moving on easier.

The old rules that applied when John Lewis began the JLP still apply now: give customers everything they want, and they'll come back and enjoy the pleasure of buying from you again.

My time at the JLP taught me what I already suspected: that one of the very best forms of earthly bliss is working to bring to customers what they want. Nowadays, I would say that what I learnt at the JLP underpins every aspect of my professional life in my work as a management consultant with a particular specialisation in helping any kind of organisation – whether in the private or public sector – become customer-centric.

The point is, VASH works, whatever product or service you are selling, whether it's Harry Potter, haricot beans, pots, conjuring services, or absolutely anything else.

As a concise summary of an attitude to customer-centricity that has been successful for close to one and a half centuries, since John Lewis founded his organisation, VASH is a great way of remembering what you need to do to keep your customers happy.

Majestic Wine

Steve Lewis, a passionate believer in *people* being at the heart of his organisation's commitment to customer-centricity, is chief executive of Majestic Wine. The company, which employs about 900 people, is today the UK's largest wine specialist by the mixed case.

Majestic Wine is a plc and listed on the AIM investment market. Benefiting in its rapid growth since the early 1990s from the greatly increased interest in wine among British consumers, Majestic currently has 161 stores in the UK, three in northern France, and annual sales of about £250 million. From the outset, the business model for the company was based around the mixed-case principle: that is, the stores did not sell single bottles.

Originally the minimum purchase was twelve bottles, though the bottles could and can be any that Majestic sells: the range includes wines, champagnes and spirits. In September 2009, the minimum number of bottles sold per purchase was reduced to six. This reduction has made Majestic more accessible to both existing and new customers and Majestic has seen a significant increase in the expansion of its customer base.

The mixed-case business model means individual sales transactions tend to be relatively large: the current average is about £122. The nature of the business model naturally puts a big premium on the importance of the quality of the customer experience. The stores tend to be spacious, attractive but fairly utilitarian in appearance, yet staffed by people who are really interested in wine and who come across as genuinely interested in helping customers and in talking about wines with them. The stores have wine-tasting areas, and the whole ambience and lay-out is arranged to enrich the customer experience.

Meeting Steve Lewis is a pleasant surprise. One never quite knows what to expect when meeting a business leader, especially not when the business leader is a retailer. After all, some retailers began running market stalls and take a pride in still coming across as being like market-stall retailers today. Steve didn't start his career running a market stall, but he did begin at Majestic Wine, his first job following university. He gained a Degree in Modern History at University College London, and he started as a trainee manager on the shop floor at Majestic Wine's Clapham store. 'When I began there back in 1985 it was the highest-turnover Majestic store,' he says, 'and it still is.'

Steve Lewis has a very noticeable and understandable pride in a career that has seen him work his way up to a position where he now runs an enormously successful company. Yet he retains his sheer enjoyment of being a retailer, and he still very much enjoys helping out when visiting stores, even loading customers' car boots! Steve aims to visit each store at least once a year.

As he says: 'At Majestic, we start with a huge advantage because we sell wine, and people who love wine love to shop for it. This means that when customers come to the shop they're already in a good mood. Our job is to develop that good mood into a truly great customer experience. This requires sincerity, a real fondness for customers and, above all, staff who have the right kind of personality to do this job. That's why I attribute much of our success to our approach to recruiting the right people.'

And he adds: 'My contribution to Majestic has been helping with the creation of a genuinely customer-focused culture. We really are a people business. Many businesses say this and don't really mean it, but we do. The problem with some people in retail is that they don't actually *like* their customers. They see them as an interruption to their working day, and they don't get a buzz out of looking after them and giving them what they want. I can't see any point working in retail if you're not going to be charming with your customers and if you're not taking a genuine pleasure in seeing them happy. Otherwise, yes, why be in this business at all? Especially, I might add, if you're selling wine, which is such a big positive part of people's lives.'

It seems we've reached a significant moment in the interview. 'Over the past twenty years or so,' Steve adds, 'people in Britain have become interested in food and wine in a way that was close to unimaginable in the past. The process has been spurred on by jet travel, foreign holidays, increasing affluence and a realisation of the sheer pleasure that food and wine bring to life. Nowadays, the restaurants of London, for example, are as good as any in Paris, and the British adaptability to the pleasures of food and drink has been a major cultural change in how we live. Look at all the TV programmes about food and drink. Look at how celebrated celebrity chefs have become. Look at the newspaper and magazine coverage of food and wine. We at Majestic love wine ourselves and we actively want to help our customers enjoy it.'

Steve also emphasises: 'We recruit people who love retail and who are really enthusiastic about taking part in it.'

Majestic has a policy of recruiting graduates. As Steve Lewis explains: 'When it comes to selecting our graduate recruits, we make the decisions based on whether we think the potential recruit is a charming kind of person who will get on with our customers and enjoy giving them great service. I don't think you can teach people to be charming. You can teach people to follow certain procedures, but charm is something they either have or they don't. You have to be many other things too, in this business – driven, focused and intelligent, for example – but charm is absolutely essential and without it I don't think we can make someone into an employee we'd be happy to employ or – and of course this is an extremely important point too – who'd be likely to be happy to work for us.'

Steve Lewis even goes as far as saying he has a litmus test for Majestic staff. 'I don't want to recruit anyone I wouldn't want to spend an hour in a car with. That seems a pretty reliable and useful indicator to me. As for hiring directors, the test there would be if I'd be happy to have them in my own home.'

Steve Lewis explains that once he's recruited staff, he makes it a policy to give them the opportunity to really enjoy their new careers and to excel in them. 'Every new recruit immediately joins an induction course and I'm the first person who addresses them. My aim is to encourage them to be all they can be when working for us. We don't incentivise staff on specific products, because we want to give them the opportunity to meet customers' needs from our entire range. And, from the very start, we build into our recruits our core philosophy, which is that we want our customers to walk out of the store having always had a great experience.'

Retail can, of course, be an extremely busy and stressful business, but Steve Lewis wants his colleagues on the shop-floor to avoid getting in a stressed state that interferes with the quality of their performance. 'Our customers tend to be cash-rich and time-poor, and we have to be careful not to let any stress we may ourselves be feeling interfere with the pleasure they have in their shopping experience.'

He recalls: 'One of my formative memories from my early days working for Majestic was when I was too keyed up one day and was helping a customer load a case of wine into her car. I thought my inner state of mind was something I was keeping private, but suddenly the customer asked me, "Are you always as angry as this?" It was a shock, and forced me to realise that we can't hide our tensions from our customers. We need to be customer-focused without being stressed and worked up about it.'

Many people in business – especially chief executives – don't necessarily behave in a way that makes you think they're putting their stated business philosophy into practice. However, Majestic Wine's head office, located on an industrial estate near Watford, is – indeed – an oasis of charm. Inside, it's full of floor-to-ceiling glass walls, agreeable pastel-coloured carpets, and a general ambience that is strangely devoid of stress and full of focused yet not frenetic people. You find yourself in a place staffed by good-looking young men and women who like working together and who enjoy their mission to collaborate in giving customers a great experience.

Steve Lewis readily acknowledges that he is running a business full of young people. 'I'm forty-seven,' he says, 'and that makes me one of the oldest people who work here.'

In a glass-walled meeting room, he casts a friendly eye at some of his colleagues in an open-plan office down below. He points them out, mentions what they do at the organisation, and proudly emphasises that most of them began their careers in Majestic Wine at the stores. 'Our staff turnover is low by the standards of the retail industry. We do our utmost to treat our staff well, and ultimately we believe that the way we treat them is reflected in how they treat their customers. Even when someone resigns, we treat them courteously and decently; we realise that the way you treat staff who are leaving is intently noted by staff who stay. Also, at a personal level, I can't stand rudeness.'

Steve enlarges on his theme. 'I want charm to be something that infuses everything we do at Majestic Wine, and I believe it does. At Majestic we don't only want to sell to customers today; we want to keep on selling to them, and we truly want them to love shopping with us. And so we care profoundly about the customer experience not because we feel we *have* to care about it, but because we *want* to care. I admire the John Lewis approach to customer service, and I'm saying this despite – or perhaps because of – Waitrose being one of our biggest competitors.'

Steve Lewis also in effect emphasises the importance of teams in Majestic's delivery of customer-centricity to its customers. 'At a practical level, when it comes to team-building, I'm a great believer in mixed teams – about forty percent of our people are women. It's no coincidence that our rate of leave of absence due to sickness is very low; people come in to work if they possibly can because they don't want to let their fellow team members down.'

What about running Majestic Wine during recessionary conditions? 'The secret of running a business successfully during a recession is to run a great business *before* the recession. Great businesses do well even during recessions because their customers love buying from them.'

And what exactly does Steve Lewis see, overall, as his role at Majestic Wine? 'Undoubtedly this: *to set an example.* I want to inspire my colleagues to make Majestic Wine the absolutely customer-focused business I want it to be. The way we behave towards our colleagues, the way I think about our customers, the way I want the stores to be run, and the kind of experience I want our customers to have – these are all vital aspects of Majestic that I want to show by example. Selling wine is a wonderful business to be in. Every day that I've worked at Majestic Wine I've believed that this is the very best place where I *could* possibly work. I want everyone at Majestic to feel that, and I want our customers to know that's how we feel, and why.'

9

CUSTOMER-CENTRICITY IN ACTION IN THE PUBLIC SECTOR

A true story of customer-centricity transformation at Wiltshire Council

In June 2007, the Department of Community Services (DCS) at the UK local authority, Wiltshire Council, came to the conclusion that it could significantly improve the lives of people served by Wiltshire Council (the large town of Swindon in Wiltshire has its own council) by following a process of fundamentally changing the way that Wiltshire Council delivered service to the community.

The change was directed at achieving the apparently mutually incompatible aims of reducing costs and using the resources available more efficiently; i.e. delivering more for less.

The senior leadership team within the DCS recognised that the challenge of delivering this kind of transformation demanded significant skills, knowledge and experience that didn't at the time exist within the department. As consequence, the DCS commissioned a competitive tendering process directed at hiring a provider who could partner with DCS in delivering the desired outcomes and achieving and sustaining the benefits achieved.

After a careful and meticulous procurement process, the business and information technology provider, Charteris plc, was selected and appointed as the provider to deliver customer-focused changes within the Adult Social Care domain. Overall, Charteris was chosen because it was able to demonstrate the following vitally important attributes:

- expertise in working with other local authorities to deliver sustainable improvements
- a highly experienced team, many of whom have had extended careers within local authorities
- a partnership ethos – working with DCS staff to ensure that Wiltshire Council would be fully included in the change process
- a clear and decisive focus on a transfer of skills and knowledge from Charteris consultants to Wiltshire Council staff
- an approach that focuses on the needs of Wiltshire Council customers
- a full recognition of the constraints around the level of funding available to support change, and a corresponding ability to demonstrate clear value

The outcomes achieved

By the time that *The Customer-Centric You* went to press in late February 2011, Wiltshire Council had made very significant progress with the transformation programme. The involvement of Charteris is recognised at Wiltshire Council as having been instrumental in achieving this success.

A particular striking example of the success of the programme has been the outcomes delivered from what is known as the 'Focus' project, where Wiltshire Council has created a fundamentally better experience for customers of the Adult Social Care division.

The Focus project alone has yielded cumulative benefits to Wiltshire Council in excess of £1 million. Furthermore, the involvement of Charteris has already become 'cost neutral': that is, the savings occasioned by Charteris's involvement have more than paid for the cost of engaging Charteris.

Crucially, the changes that delivered these cost-savings have become embedded in the way Wiltshire Council delivers customer-centricity to its customers and in how the DCS now operates and is designed. This means that the changes will be sustainable. Just as importantly, Wiltshire Council has begun to make radical changes in its culture through the DCS – Wiltshire Council's staff are now challenging themselves to make sure that everything they do is focused on improving the lives of Wiltshire Council customers, rather than only meeting the needs of the DCS.

Already, Charteris's involvement with the DCS of Wiltshire Council has led to a significant transfer of skills, knowledge and ways of thinking to the DCS, which is now well equipped to improve its own ways of working, whether through a future change programme or in its usual business activities. For the DCS, this has been a major shift and improvement in the capability of staff and, as the DCS explains, 'is exactly what we were looking to gain from partnering with external providers, leaving us with a real legacy of competence which we believe can be transferred across the council.'

A spokesperson for the DCS adds:

'With the help of customer-centricity we are not only completely changing the way we work within Wiltshire Council but we are also influencing and shaping the means by which people even enter our processes. This is a decisive and vital shift in the way that the needs of our customers – the people who use the services of Wiltshire Council – are met. Charteris has also enabled us to develop a model of working, across the whole council, that achieves our needs to deliver the necessary cost-savings and, at the same time, to improve the lives of our customers – in a sustainable way.

'Charteris has helped us be successful by bringing us a combination of:

- strategic insight
- an approach to change that delivers real cost-savings while focusing on customer needs
- a very robust management approach to programmes that has forced us to focus on benefit delivery
- crucially, a radical change in the way that our staff think and act.

'No less crucially, Charteris has *enabled our staff to deliver the changes themselves*, which is proving highly effective in transferring skills and knowledge and ensuring that the new ways of working and thinking become part of our business as usual.

'Charteris has proved itself a provider that can truly partner with us rather than just delivering the changes to us. We greatly needed this partnership capability of Charteris as it was in effect the only way that our staff would adopt a radically different model and, which is also a crucial point to mention, will be able to keep improving it after the provider has completed the project.

'Charteris has proved that they can work with us in this way...'

A personal view of the transformation of the adult social care department of Wiltshire Council to full customer-centricity

by Sue Redmond, corporate director, community services, Wiltshire Council

When I joined Wiltshire Council in 2006 as Corporate Director of Community Services — one of five corporate directors overall — I knew I'd be jumping in at the deep end.

*I couldn't help but be aware that Wiltshire social care was in crisis as news about the difficulties it had been having was all over **The Guardian** and in the professional press too. I was really keen to join Wiltshire Council again as I'd worked there in the mid-90s and I knew what a great Council it was and I also loved Wiltshire itself. The Council had had an excellent relationship with its customers in the past; I was really keen to do what I could to solve the crisis.*

The problems Wiltshire were having had arisen from an attempt to link up the council and the local health services. The synergy wasn't working, and everyone was suffering: customers and council officials alike. It hadn't helped that there'd been an overspend of £11 million the previous year, so making savings was as crucial an objective for me as was playing my part in getting community services on the right track again.

I was braced for a tough few months in my new job, and that was a good thing, because the months certainly were tough. I had to do my best to win and rebuild trust between the council all stakeholders: in particular individual customers (I prefer this more user-friendly word to the more formal and remote 'service users') and also our partners such as the Primary Care Trust.

One of the first tasks to which the other corporate directors and I applied ourselves was to address the problem of the highly silo'd structure of Wiltshire Council. This wasn't helping at all with our imperative of simultaneously effecting a massive improvement in customer services while also saving money.

Following a plan developed by Jane Scott, leader of Wiltshire Council, we set to work re-organising the council into a silo-free corporate structure in which everyone at the council could really collaborate and co-operate as they pushed our new initiatives forward. The new budget, for example, would be managed and spent not by individual silos but by the new, restructured organisation, with the management and expenditure – again, this was Jane Scott's idea – being based around real, constructive dialogues between Wiltshire Council and its customers.

*Our overall objective was for local people to be deeply involved with deciding what services they needed. In order to put this aim into practice, we split Wiltshire Council into 20 local community areas and at once applied ourselves to working with customers at these local levels to find out what they most needed from us. These local areas **weren't** new types of silos but simply a convenient administrative way of talking to people. We soon discovered that different localities varied, sometimes more than one might have expected, in terms of the different agendas and priorities they had; I felt discovering this was a positive step because it meant that we were creating the very dialogues we wanted to create.*

I found that creating the dialogues at a local level was definitely helping to advance what I regard as my three main professional challenges, namely:

- *creating a way for the council to talk to people at a local level*
- *ensuring that people's voices are heard*
- *transforming the way adult social services are delivered to customers*

By the summer of 2007, I felt we had made considerable progress with the first two objectives, but I still felt there was still much that we needed to do with the third one. What was needed was, in my view, a pretty comprehensive restructuring of the adult social care department.

The problem was, though, that the department had been restructured many times prior to my arrival, and the resulting new structures (including the one we had by the summer of 2007) were not felt to be right for the purpose they needed to carry out. I think it fair to say that by this point there was a mistrust of management itself carrying out another restructuring. This being so, I began to wonder whether an external organisation might be able to bring us something we couldn't perhaps at that stage bring ourselves and which we certainly needed: a muscular, efficient new structure that would be completely focused around our customers' needs. We finally made the decision to find a consultancy partner who could look at how we were delivering adult social services to customers and make recommendations for transforming this.

We put this assignment out to tender, and appointed the business and IT consultancy Charteris to helping us with this. After a careful investigation of our processes and methods, they delivered their report, which they called **Focus on customers underpins success** *in the autumn of 2007.*

It made sobering reading. I had been expecting some radical suggestions, but even I was surprised to encounter the main conclusion of the Charteris report, which was that, in their view, a fairly astonishing **70 percent** *of our processes for delivering adult social care, did nothing of the kind. Instead, Charteris found that this 70 percent of processes were bound up with our agenda rather than the agenda of our customers, and so were not adding value to what we were offering to our customers.*

This was of course a most disconcerting finding, and it was little consolation to be told by Charteris that it was very often the case, elsewhere in the public and private sector, that about 70 percent or more of corporate effort is, in fact, geared around the organisation's own needs rather than those of customers. Charteris believes that the correct ratio should be that no more than 30 percent of effort should be devoted to internal matters, with the obvious corollary that 70 percent of effort needs to be focused on customers.

We accepted the findings of Charteris's report, and a process then began for putting their recommendations into practice. In broad terms Charteris recommended that we work towards the following goals:

- become outcome-focused
- achieve a culture change that puts the customer absolutely at the heart of what we do
- use 'joined-up' processes; that is, processes that are not the sole preserve of one department but which go across different departments and which are specifically designed to focus on customers
- work as constructively as feasible with partners
- embed performance management
- improve productivity

More specifically, Charteris recommended that we absolutely prioritise the need to listen to customers and then to respond to what customers want. The precise objectives Charteris recommended to us here were as follows:

- obtain an internal view of what was important to customers
- obtain the customers' view of what they need
- understand the difference between Wiltshire's view and what the customer needs
- use this different view to align Wiltshire with the customer and develop design principles for use in the 'to be' state

These design principles were:

- right information at the right time
- design principles for the majority, not the exception
- empower people to deal with exceptions
- appropriate use of resources by setting a target of 70:30 'value add' in all we do – in other words, at least 70 percent of

our efforts should add value to the customer, with a maximum of our efforts being focused on our own agenda.

- *clearly and concisely state the 'why', the 'how' and the 'when' in all communications – this methodology is a powerful precaution against any tendency to vagueness in our correspondence with customers; every letter or other communication we send out will state **why** we are sending it, how the matter at hand will help the customer, and **when** the customer can expect us to have delivered what is necessary.*

It wasn't possible to put the recommendations into practice overnight. The overall aim was nothing less than a complete transformation of how Wiltshire Council delivers social care services to adults, and this has naturally required a change process involving further investigation and the setting of tasks and objectives, as well as a piloting process. The time-frame before we were ready to roll out the full transformation – it began to be rolled out in April 2009 and the roll-out was substantially completed at the end of November 2009 – may seem like a long time, and indeed in private sector terms probably would be.

However, we needed to gauge and test the forward momentum of what we were doing, and educate our 400 staff in what we were doing, as well as – naturally – maintain our services to customers during this period.

In essence, what the roll-out has involved is nothing less than a complete restructuring of our teams, of the management of these teams and of how Wiltshire Council staff work together. A special priority has been placed on the role of the customer co-ordinator (often known internally as the 'navigator') who helps customers move through our processes in order to get the best result for the customer. The first phone call the customer makes to us is regarded as particularly important and we believe we have now become adept at listening to customers, especially during that first phone call, and taking responsibility for addressing customers' problems.

We also pay particular attention to avoid a situation where the customer is just being tossed from one department to another. We don't do that; we focus on using the initial phone call to help the customer using all our departments available.

It's been very gratifying that in March 2009 we received a local government award for connecting communities and were given the national award of being considered a beacon among local authorities. Even more gratifying was the fact that other councils have acknowledged that they can learn from us. Managers involved in social care from Kent, Warrington and Fife council have visited us over the past few months to find out more about our work.

The benefits to our customers are clear: this new structure has not been imposed as a 'top-down' structure but has been created from the first to minister to what customers really want and has been substantially specified by the very front-line staff who talk to customers every day when customers phone in.

Indeed, the way we handle that first phone call is a vital part of the new structure and the way we do things now. We place a great emphasis now on getting absolutely as much information as we can about the customers' needs from that very first phone call. We place just as much emphasis on getting feedback from customers about what they think of what we are doing for them.

As far as specific benefits to our customers are concerned, I think something of the flavour of the success of what we've been doing can be gauged from looking at some numbers, which include:

- Since we began the new way of doing things at Wiltshire, nearly 4,000 local people have attended Area Board meetings in Wiltshire and attendances continue to grow.
- More than 10,000 local people have now signed up to be involved with work of the Boards through local community area networks.
- More than £200,000 has been awarded to support local community projects.
- Police, Fire and Rescue, NHS and MOD are fully engaged with our work and attend meetings regularly.
- More than 75 percent of parish and town councils have attended Area Board meetings.

- *We have achieved a 75 percent satisfaction rating for Area Board meetings that take place in many of the areas surveyed. There is also a clear indication that this rating is improving.*
- *Issues have been logged on the Area Boards Issues System and more than a third have been resolved during the last cycle.*
- *Young people are engaged at two-thirds of Area Boards meetings through the local CAYPIGs (Community Area Young People's Issues Groups).*
- *Improved audio/visual support and loop system now available with trained technician.*
- *Community speedwatch bid launched through the area boards to deal with widespread local concerns.*

*Perhaps most significantly of all, our new key performance indicators now relate above all to the outcomes we achieve **for people**.*

My experience at Wiltshire is that taking every step to put into practice the vital rule – that a minimum of 70 percent of our efforts goes towards our customers' agenda and a maximum of 30 percent of our efforts goes into our own agenda – is the way to achieve the maximum happiness and satisfaction for customers.

10

KEY ADVICE AND GUIDELINES CONTAINED IN THIS BOOK

Please note:
1. These pieces of advice and guidelines are presented in the chronological order that they appear in the book.
2. It has been necessary to edit some of the advice and guidelines for this chapter, as here they appear out of context compared with how they appear in the text above.

- *A customer is any person, anywhere and in any capacity, whom you want to influence to want what you are offering them.*

- *You yourself* will be infinitely more fulfilled, satisfied and happy in your life when you are genuinely switched on to the agenda of others, and have learned to care about that agenda because you *want* to care about it.

- The importance of customer-centricity is even greater during a time of economic challenges.

- You can never know too much about what your customers need, and you can never stop finding the best ways to meet those needs.

- You can't improve your relationships with your customers in any meaningful sense by just following a set of guidelines.

- Being customer-centric is especially important when your life is difficult: whether or not the difficulties you are going through stem completely or partly from problems at work.

- Generally, when our lives are difficult we tend to act in a more selfish way, but on the whole we are more likely so solve our problems if we become *less* selfish and focus more on the agenda of other people.

- Merely influencing someone to *like* what you are offering them is not enough. No-one is going to buy something from you merely because they like it; they have to feel they need it, and they are only going to part with their hard-earned cash to buy what you offering them if they really *do* feel they need it.

- We all need to keep our relationships with our customers, in every area of our lives, in a constant state of repair.

- *A customer is any person, anywhere and in any capacity, whom you want to influence to want what you are offering them.*

- It is extremely difficult, if not close to impossible, for anyone to become truly customer-centric if they see themselves as having two essentially distinct personas: their business persona and their 'personal life' persona.

- The higher you progress in your career, the more important your personality becomes compared with your technical skills.

- Understanding precisely *who your customers really are* is (of course) a vitally important process, but it's just as important to understand *what your customers are really getting from you.*

- Psychological gratification is in fact the prime benefit of many products and services. It follows that the more the organisation knows about these psychological gratifications, the more likely it is to be successful in selling its products and services to customers.

- Most organisations selling specific products and services to customers probably most likely have more extensive opportunities than they might imagine to embody – in their marketing and advertising activity – their knowledge of what their customers really get from their products and services.

- If your great aim is that the customers in all the different areas of your life actively want what you're offering them (and, if they're commercial customers, are willing to buy it from you), you must find within yourself the energy, discipline and imagination to see the world from your customers' point of view and then (most likely) adjust your behaviour towards your customers, and the nature of what you're offering them, accordingly.

- *Customer-centricity is an attribute of any entity that is doing all that it can reasonably do to focus on, and minister to, the agenda of its customers.*

- Charteris's definition of customer-centricity is:

  the process of ensuring that every individual and department within an organisation is taking every step feasible to add value to what the organisation does for its customers.

- All business activity on the planet is designed to meet *human needs*. Even business activity directed around providing food for the animals at a zoo, or indeed for your pet dog or cat, is really directed around the needs of the people who run the zoo, or around the needs of the owner of the pet. Business is a human phenomenon, not an animal phenomenon.

- Within the world of business – which of course embraces products and services delivered by public services organisations as well as by profit-making organisations – added value is:

  the benefit, perceived by the customer, that a customer gains from a particular product or service above and beyond the intrinsic 'face value' of that product.

- At a technical level, added value is something we can see, hear, feel, smell, touch or are aware of psychologically and emotionally and which we see as important to us and improving our lives.

- A *need* is something that genuinely improves a customer's life. A *want* is something the customer desires, or think he or she does.

- A customer may say they want something when in fact what they need is something different. The difference between a perceived need and a perceived want arises from:
  - a lack of information on the part of the customer
  - the fact that customers often make decisions based on emotions rather than logic

- As providers of customer-centricity, it is our job to know what the customer really needs.

- The overall relationship between added value and customer-centricity is this: *if your customers don't attach a conceptualised added value to the products or services you are offering them then you can't possibly be customer-centric.*

- Hewett's First Law is: *No organisation can be customer-centric unless it is devoting at least 70 percent of its efforts and energies exclusively to the agenda of its customers.*

- The only realistic way for an organisation that wants to be continually customer-centric to proceed is to *be, as far as possible, constantly aware of the nature of the changing demand, and to strive at all times to be able to answer the question 'where and how am I adding value for this customer?'*

- All the same, cost is too often used by organisations as an excuse for not performing well on the customer-centricity front. After all, the organisation is in business to serve its customers, and if it is in effect saying *'intense competition in our markets makes it too expensive for us to serve our customers properly'* then it should look at ways of streamlining its activities in order to reduce its costs so that it *can* serve its customers properly. Otherwise the very fact that there *is* intense competition in its sector is likely to drive it out of business.

- Two things can indeed be very much alike and yet utterly different. Heaven and hell really can be in the same place; *it all depends on the attitude and the governing sensibility that prevail there.*

- Even the most customer-centric of us have moods and times when we do not feel inclined to be warm to people. Of course, we need to understand these moods and prevent them from influencing our behaviour.

- What *is* ridiculous – and tragic – is that so many people persist, against not only the interests of other people but even against their own interests, to *have little or no inherent interest in the agenda of strangers at all, and are too blind to that agenda to realise that this indifference is generally the biggest reason why they don't fulfil themselves either professionally or in a personal sense.*

- When it comes to implementing customer-centricity in an organisation, technology will only be effective if the organisation has first properly restructured itself and reorganised itself at a practical, conceptual and customer-focused level.

- Don't be misled into thinking that what your customers want from you is necessarily the product or service you are selling. What they really want from you may very well be something more general: a need that the product or service only meets in a limited way at present.

- The overall objective for which an organisation should aim is a re-structuring of the organisation that results in every person actively involved with the organisation in any way doing everything they can to further customer-centricity within the organisation.

- A stick of rock is about as customer-centric a thing as it's possible to imagine. It delivers its welcome, its sweetness, its flavour throughout its entire being, and for many people biting into it and wondering if your teeth will survive the experience is all part of the fun.

- The message that runs through the entire stick of rock is exactly like the role customer-centricity should play within an organisation. Every part of the organisations should be infused with the same belief in customer-centricity that is being put into practice in everything the organisation does.

- Organisations should use their human, capital, know-how, operational and technological resources to create the 'stick of rock' effect throughout their entire organisation, with the effect being not to deliver the stick of rock's message but rather comprehensive customer-centricity.

- In the case of customer-centricity, there are two killer applications. These are:
    - selling
    - cost reduction

- The great thing about these two killer 'apps' is that, *if customer-centricity is properly applied within an organisation, the organisation can enjoy the benefits of extra sales and cost reductions.*

- The very process of implementing customer-centricity creates a streamlining within an organisation that should ideally introduce the highest levels of customer focus into all the processes and activities of the organisation, which, if properly engineered, should indeed yield increased sales at reduced costs.

- Hewett's Second Law is: *customer-centricity is the holy grail of all professional activities because, properly implemented, it can lead to the winning of additional revenue as well as cost reductions.*

A YOUNG CUSTOMER WRITES...

Where should customer-centricity head in the future if it is to meet the needs of the young people who will be the adult customers of the decades heading towards the middle of the twenty-first century and beyond.

What follows is what Imogen Chitty thinks about this. Imogen was sixteen years old when she wrote the following:

My life as a teenage consumer

by Imogen Chitty

I'm sixteen and love shopping, which – especially when it's shopping for clothes – I mostly do with my friends. Actually, while I enjoy internet shopping on websites that I find fun, accessible, user-friendly and relevant to my needs, I do far more of my shopping in actual stores than on the internet. Shops I especially like are Top Shop – the chain of clothes shops – and a big department store called Ely's in Wimbledon near my house.

Of course I am very familiar with the internet and with internet shopping too: I suppose I've been using the internet since I was about eight or nine.

I think most stores I actually visit in person treat me pretty well; though I'd agree with a friend of mine (who's about my own age) who says that she thinks some shops don't take young people too seriously as they know that young people don't have a lot of money.

*When I **do** decide to buy something from the internet, what I want most of all is quick and easy access: if it's not easy for me to shop at a particular website then most likely I won't.*

As a teenage girl I've grown up using the internet on an almost daily basis. Half an hour after arriving home from school I'll already have checked my Facebook profile, skimmed through the BBC news homepage, researched a school project and started my homework. When I do internet shopping, I want to be able to do it at the same kind of speed. I don't want to spend ages trawling through pages and pages of products. As far as I'm concerned, internet shopping is not for browsing, it's for convenience. If I can't find what I want within a maximum of six clicks, the website has got some redesigning to do.

I am glad to say that there are a few websites which have really tapped into the teenage mindset. iTunes is a perfect example of a site which combines speed and ease of access with creating an experience. The search features are unparalleled, and I know I will quickly find almost anything I want. The website is kept up to date with what's current and what's popular, and the personalisation is amazing. iTunes directs itself towards me and what I want. The 'Genius' toolbar throws up suggestions of songs I may like based on my previous purchases, which means I can discover new sounds and artists suited to my tastes. Personalisation is a theme which every shop should aim at and strive towards. It really is what makes the difference between a good shopping experience and a really great one.

Physical shopping is a different story, and, for me, as I say most definitely a recreational activity. My favourite shops are those which make shopping fun, and create an 'experience'. If you feel you are a part of the 'world' of that shop, you are much more inclined to spend your money there. For example, shops where you are allowed to test out products or have a go at using them are great – you actually get a feel for the product and the message you get is that the retailer trusts you. This trust will be remembered when you are considering a purchase.

One of the best experiences I've had shopping was when a clothes retailer offered a free 'personal shopper' service – there was no pressure to buy, yet I still did, as the shop had taken the time to make the whole thing an individual experience for me, and really advised me well. They offered suggestions based on the things I said I liked, and again the personalisation of the experience was the most memorable part.

In contrast, there are some high street shops which just miss this point. Over-branding means that you can be made to feel that it's all about the company and its image, not the your own style and preferences. Often, if a shop sells purely based on its name, the clothes all look very similar and all originality is removed. This may work for younger teens who often want to be 'part of the crowd', but its appeal fades as you get older and are trying as hard as you can to be individual. At sixteen, we are just beginning to have more spending power, maybe due to an allowance or a part time job.

We also have clear ideas of what we want to spend our money on. I recently went to a brand-focused high fashion store and asked for a catalogue; I was told that I had to be over 18 to buy it, as it contained nude images, and it also cost a massive £9.99 to buy. The shop had completely missed its target audience – primarily under 18s. What's more, no one wants to have to buy a catalogue, when everyone else is giving them out free.

Social networking plays a big part in young people's lives and sites such as Facebook are great for broadcasting information to a large number of people. However, I and most other people my age use Facebook to keep in touch with friends and for information about upcoming events, so shop advertisements on Facebook would not be hugely appreciated. There are of course Facebook 'pages' for shops, but these are not particularly useful as you can't browse for many items and cannot buy them, and I would just use the website if I was online anyway. What would be a good idea for shops to do is instead of advertising products, to advertise events, sales or offers coming up which may draw people to go shopping.

Maybe the way forward is to allow young customers to have more of a say about what they want to see on the shelves and on the web? Ideally, teenage consumers should be able to put forward their own concepts and designs. In fashion, for example, we would like a wider range of shapes and styles. I can almost always tell where one of my friends' items of clothing has come from, and people often end up wearing the same things. We want to be different and original, and it's currently hard to do that. We need a voice and a forum, a dialogue where our ideas are listened to and *where we are made to feel that our views matter. I think any shop – whether physical, internet-based or both – that makes us feel **that** is really going to succeed!*

AFTERWORD

J.B. Priestley's great play, *An Inspector Calls,* was first produced in 1945, just a year before *It's a Wonderful Life* was made.

Priestley's play, written at the end of World War II but set in 1912 – just before the 33 years of political disaster in Europe and beyond that led to two world wars – is about a pompous, self-satisfied, uncaring, upper-middle-class British family that consists of a mother, father, daughter, son and the daughter's prospective husband.

One evening, after having enjoyed a good dinner, they're visited by a mysterious 'inspector' whom they assume, possibly incorrectly, to be a police inspector but who may instead be playing a more mythic, even close to religious, role in the story. Gradually, the family come to the appalled realisation that they have each played a role in precipitating the suicide of a lonely, beautiful, girl called Eva Smith.

The inspector's parting words to the family seem to me to sum up the essence of what it truly means to think in a customer-centric way:

> But just remember this. One Eva Smith has gone – but there are millions and millions and millions of Eva Smiths and John Smiths still left with us, with their lives, their hopes and fears, their suffering and chance of happiness, all intertwined with our lives, and what we think and say and do. We don't live alone. We are members of one body. We are responsible for each other. And I tell you that the time will soon come when, if men will not learn that lesson, then they will be taught it in fire and blood and anguish.

Reader, let's learn that lesson. Let's never forget it. Let's see customer-centricity not only as a strategy for making our professional lives and personal lives more successful, but as a way of ensuring that, when in the fullness of time we depart from the community of human beings, that community will be all the better for us having lived in it.

THE END

INDEX